AF317052

WOMAN AT THE WELL WALKING BY FAITH

How to trust in God

By

Christian Ceasar

ISBN
Paperback: 979-8-90427-011-7
Hardback: 979-8-90427-012-4

Dedication

This book is dedicated to every person who has ever felt overlooked, overwhelmed, or uncertain about their path

To the also who cried in silence, for battles, no one saw and still chose to keep going, this is for you.

I dedicate this to the believers who refused to give up, even when life gets heavy. May these words remind you that your situation does not define you, your faith does

Acknowledgment

I give honor and glory to God, Who's grace , Mercy and guidance carried me through every chapter of this journey. Without him, none of this would be possible.

To my family and loved ones, thank you for waving support and prayers, and encouragement. You stood by me through every season, reminding me to keep going even when it wasn't easy.

And to every challenge, setback, and difficult situations I face thank you. You didn't break me you built me. You strengthen my faith and reminding me that through God, every situation can turn into a blessing.

About the author

Christian Caesar is an aspiring author entrepreneur and visionary behind the Empowering brand Bos$ BLESS OVER SITUATIONS. Through faith, resilience and personal growth, Christian uses her voice to uplift motivate others to rise Above life's challenges

With a deep passion to encourage others, she transforms real life experiences into a powerful message of strength, purpose, and elevation. Her work is rooted in faith and designed to remind people that no matter what they faith, they are chosen, steel, covered, and steel capable of greatness.

Christian Caesar's mission is to inspire individuals to walk bowling and purpose. Trust God's plan and turn every situation into a testimony blessing.

Table of Contents

Hey there, Amazing Reader!

Welcome aboard this incredible journey called faith! You hold in your hands a devotional that's not just a collection of words, but an invitation to dive deep into the ocean of your spiritual life. Think of it as your personal guidebook, designed to spark inspiration, ignite reflections, and stir up a passion for trusting God even when life throws you curveballs. Let's get real—faith is not always straightforward; it's messy, unpredictable, and sometimes downright challenging. However, each day, we have a unique chance to pause and reflect, to explore how faith can ripple through our everyday lives. From the moment I felt called to write this book, I dreamed of creating something that encourages you to open your heart and mind to the powerful messages hidden in scripture and daily reflection.

Each of the thirty entries in this devotional is crafted to touch on a specific aspect of faith and trust in God. Consider this an adventure through various themes that resonate with our spiritual journeys, like 'The Well of Trust' where we'll journey together exploring the biblical wisdom of the Woman at the Well. She's a powerful reminder that there's an abundance of faith waiting for us if we dare to explore it!

Then we'll dive into 'Embracing Uncertainty'—life can be chaotic and unpredictable, right? Together, we'll learn how to navigate these uncertainties while holding God's hand. And oh, have I mentioned daily surrender? Yes, who wouldn't want to drop those heavy burdens at the feet of our Creator? So let's discover how to let go of anxieties that weigh us down!

Every day, we'll draw from scripture, infuse personal anecdotes, and establish actionable steps that keep our faith alive and vibrant. That's right! We're not just going to reflect—we're going to ACT! Whether you need a nudge to put your faith into practice or want to celebrate the little victories of life, these devotions are packed with encouragement, community, and powerful insights to guide you along the way.

But wait, there's more! We'll confront doubt together, because guess what? It's a part of faith too! The 'Skeptic' represents that voice in your head questioning everything. By addressing doubt head on, we'll build a more robust faith, one that stands strong in the face of challenges. How invigorating to discover faith as a lifelong journey that's worth every step of the way!

I am beyond excited to share with you ways to cultivate a spirit of gratitude, recognizing God's hand in our lives even amid struggles. 'Faith in Action' will inspire you to take those leaps into the unknown, while 'Finding Peace in Prayer' offers you sacred time to simply connect with Him.

Let's emphasize the importance of community! Surrounding ourselves with fellow believers is like holding hands on our journey—encouragement and support are essential. So, buckle up for this joyful exploration, for we will foster deeper connections not just with God, but with each other as we step together into the unknown. Each page is woven together to create a tapestry of experiences meant to inspire and uplift.

As you read through this book, I encourage you to dive deep—grab a journal, jot down your thoughts, pray through the prompts, and engage with each reflection wholeheartedly. Whether you're new to faith or seasoned in your walk with God, this book is a companion meant to help you draw nearer to Him. I'm thrilled to share this journey and can't wait for you to experience the uplifting power of faith. Trust the process, embrace the adventure, and let's journey together!

So, dear friend, I'm eager for you to devour these pages and uncover profound insights that await you. Let's embark on this journey of faith together, and I promise you'll come out the other side feeling inspired and transformed. This isn't just a read; it's a sacred conversation with your heart and spirit.

With excitement to share this adventure, With heart and enthusiasm, Christian Ceasar

The Well of Trust

Foundations of Faith

The sun was high in the sky, casting a warm glow over the village of Sychar as the Woman at the Well approached the familiar site. This well, which served as a gathering place for her community, seemed to hold the weight of her past, her identity, and her unspoken fears. Today, however, something felt different, as if the air itself was charged with anticipation. She had been coming to this well for years, filling her jug with water, but today was poised to become a transformative encounter.

Drawing closer to the well, she noticed a man sitting there. He was a stranger, not someone from her village or the surrounding area. The sight of him stirred an inexplicable mix of curiosity and caution within her. She carried the weight of societal judgment, the whispers and stares that followed her wherever she went. This man's presence disrupted the routine of her life and her understanding of the world.

"Will you give me a drink?" he asked, startling her from her thoughts. His voice was gentle yet filled with authority, drawing her into a moment of unexpected connection.

"Why are you talking to me, a Samaritan woman?" she replied, skepticism lacing her words. The rigid boundaries of race, gender, and social norms shaped her response, reminding her that asking for help—especially from a man like him—could never end well. She had learned to expect rejection.

"If you knew the gift of God and who it is that asks you for a drink, you would have asked him, and he would have given you living water," he responded, his eyes locking onto hers with an intensity that disarmed her skepticism.

Living water? The phrase twisted in her mind, stirring a longing she had buried deep within her. She was familiar with the wells of her life, both physical and emotional. They were places of necessity, yet they were also places steeped in disappointment, unfulfilled dreams, and unacknowledged pain. A part of her wanted to laugh at his words—they felt ridiculous. Who could promise something as profound as living water?

"Sir," she said, her voice betraying an edge of sarcasm, "you have nothing to draw with, and the well is deep. Where can you get this living water?" She looked down into the well, making an unspoken tradition of her cynicism evident as she considered the depths of her yearning alongside the physical depths of the well.

The conversation unfolded, layer by layer, revealing the rawness of her life. He spoke of an endless source of satisfaction that would banish her thirst permanently. Her heart quickened as she processed his offer, a flicker of hope igniting within her gut amid the shadows of doubt. As he delved into her past, revealing intimate details she dared not speak, she found herself paralyzed between fear and desire—fear of exposure versus the deep-seated desire to be truly known and understood.

"Go, call your husband and come back," he said, exposing the secret she held like a fragile shard of glass; a secret that had trapped her in a cycle of shame. Her companions in the village had long branded her due to her past relationships, her failures drawing invisible lines that she could not cross. In that moment, the ache of rejection pulsed like a heartbeat in her chest.

"I have no husband," she replied, her voice barely above a whisper.

"You are right when you say you have no husband. The fact is, you have had five husbands, and the man you now have is not your husband. What you have said is quite true," he said, speaking not with condemnation but with an understanding that seemed to pierce through her defenses.

As he spoke, a wave of understanding washed over her—he saw her completely, and yet he offered her neither condemnation nor dismissal. In that moment, the walls she had built crumbled, one brick at a time. The weight of societal judgment and her own self-loathing began to lift as she confronted the truth of her existence—she was a woman, flawed yet worthy, weary yet yearning. Trust, she realized, was a slippery thing, challenging for her to grasp.

Trust breeds faith, and it was in this moment that she began to comprehend the foundational nature of faith built on trust. She stood on shaky ground, aware that this man was offering her more than just water; he was offering a new identity—an invitation to transform her life and her story. This invitation was not just for her; it echoed through the ages, reaching every heart that has ever felt the despair of inadequacy.

"Sir, I can see that you are a prophet," she said, the words tumbling from her lips as she tried to redirect the conversation. The comfort of belief soon collided with the reality of her past. Questions surfaced in her mind—would this man truly accept her? Could he lead her towards something better?

The man—this stranger—had become a mirror reflecting her deepest fears and longings. They spoke of worship, grace, and the true nature of God, revealing how misunderstandings could shape faith and belief systems. The significance of trusting God beyond societal expectations and norms began to seep into her understanding. He was dismantling the barriers she had constructed around her heart.

In that profound exchange, a seed was planted—a foundation upon which her faith could grow. No longer was she bound by the labels others placed upon her; her trust began to anchor her belief. She felt hope shifting within her, unfurling in the sincerity of his words.

"Come, see a man who told me everything I ever did. Could this be the Messiah?" she exclaimed, a newfound authenticity driving her spirit. It wasn't simply her words; it was the revelation that spread through her soul—the transformation that came from embracing trust and yielding to the divine presence before her. This is the essence of faith—a willingness to step beyond what we know and walk into the unknown with open hearts.

The disciples returned, surprised to find the two of them speaking. Yet the Woman at the Well was no longer defined by societal expectations. She felt a voice rising within her, propelling her to share the truth she had encountered. In that moment, faced with the reality of both her past and her newfound understanding, she made a choice to trust—trust in the man who gave her living water, thereby embarking on the journey of faith that would carry her forward.

Her story resonates with so many—those who grapple with their own identity and self-worth. Readers, too, may find themselves standing at their wells of doubt and fear, questioning the stability of their trust in God. The struggle of faith is often intertwined with uncertainty; the very essence of doubt can shake even the strongest believer. But the Woman at the Well's encounter serves as a reminder of the power of revelation and connection. Trust is built through vulnerability and an open heart.

Scripture states in Proverbs 3:5-6, "Trust in the Lord with all your heart and lean not on your own understanding; in all your ways submit to him, and he will make your paths straight." These words invite us into a posture of faith, where the foundations of trust are laid down in the willingness to release control. It beckons us to confront our fears, to live authentically, and to seek understanding beyond surface-level beliefs.

As we navigate the complexities of faith, it's vital to recognize the areas where our trust in God may need strengthening. Much like the Woman at the Well, we are encouraged to examine our internal landscapes and consider the societal messages that shape our perceptions of ourselves, our relationships, and our connection to God. There may be parts of our lives that feel fractured or uncertain—places where doubt holds sway.

Practical steps to identify these areas of need begin with reflection. Consider journaling about those moments in your life where you felt your faith falter or where trust seemed elusive. Guiding questions could include:

What situations have led me to doubt my worthiness before God?

Are there past experiences that continue to shape my view of trust and relationships?

How can I confront the barriers that prevent me from embracing faith fully?

In examining these questions, take time to sit in prayer, inviting God to bring clarity and confidence to your reflections. Be mindful that trust is not a singular event, but a journey—a continuous act of faith requiring courage and commitment. Just as the Woman at the Well stepped into the unknown with a heart open to transformation, so too can we take steps toward fortifying our trust in God.

Additionally, consider engaging with your faith community. Sharing your experiences of doubt and uncertainty can create spaces for healing and encouragement. See how those around you have navigated their struggles and what lessons they have learned. By hearing stories of others, you may find inspiration to deepen your own trust.

If you find yourself grappling with areas of unforgiveness or feelings of shame, meditate on the promises of Scripture, allowing the truth to wash over you. Romans 15:13 offers hope in abundance: "May the God of hope fill you with all joy and peace as you trust in him, so that you may overflow with hope by the power of the Holy Spirit." Embrace this hope, recalling moments where faith has transformed uncertainty into assurance.

Through the story of the Woman at the Well, we are reminded that the foundations of faith are built on trust. Trust in God allows us to confront our fears, embrace our truths, and step into the fullness of who we are created to be. As we move forward, may we reflect upon our own wells of trust, drawing upon the life-giving water offered to us through faith—and in doing so, may we each find the strength to believe, to hope, and to share the story of grace that emerges from our journeys.

The Well as a Metaphor

In our lives, we often navigate through moments of uncertainty, joy, despair, and hope. Each of these experiences brings us closer to understanding the essence of trust and faith. The metaphor of the well serves as a profound symbol for the depths of faith and the sustenance it offers. Just as a physical well provides water—the essential element for life—our spiritual well holds the promise of profound connection and support, particularly in our times of need.

The well is a source of life. In many cultures, it has served as a central gathering place, where communities come together to draw water and share stories. It is a space imbued with significance, where physical needs are met alongside emotional and spiritual exchanges. Similarly, our well of trust is a space we can return to, especially when life's trials become overwhelming. It is in this well that we cultivate our ability to trust in God, nourish our relationships, and find peace amidst chaos.

Drawing from the well of trust requires an intentional act of faith. Over the years, I have experienced moments of clarity and peace that have stemmed from deepening my relationship with God. One instance stands out: during a particularly tumultuous phase in my life, filled with uncertainty regarding my career path, I found myself feeling desolate and overwhelmed. It was amidst this despair that I felt compelled to revisit my well—a familiar spot where I would spend time in prayer and reflection.

As I sat at the edge of this well, I allowed myself to pour out my feelings of fear and doubt. In that moment, I felt the weight of my worries lift, as if the very waters of the well were washing over them. I vividly recall the peace that enveloped me—a sense of reassurance that I was not alone in my struggles. The well had become a reservoir of comfort, reminding me that, like the water within it, faith could flow freely in the face of adversity.

Reflecting on my experience, I realized how vital it is to draw from our wells of trust regularly. Life can often provoke waves of questions: "Am I worthy?" "What if I fail?" "Will I ever be enough?" These doubts act like stones that obstruct our access to the well, blocking the flow of faith in our lives. Fear can create a barrier, obscuring the truth of who we are and who God is. It can seize us in tight grips, forbidding us from venturing closer to that sacred source of sustenance.

It is essential to recognize these barriers for what they are—temporary obstacles that can be overcome. The moment I confront my fears and doubts, acknowledging them as part of my journey, I find that I can begin to shift my perspective. One day, during a small group gathering centered around trust, a fellow believer shared their insight on fear. They spoke of it as a natural response but emphasized the importance of not allowing it to dictate our relationship with God. This perspective deeply resonated with me, encouraging me to face my fears head-on and align my focus on the promises woven throughout scripture.

Like the well, our individual wells of trust are not always accessible at first glance. Sometimes, we must dig deeper, exploring the hidden layers of our hearts. As we venture into the depths, we may unearth aspects of our faith that remain dormant—thoughts and feelings buried beneath the weight of daily anxieties. It can be through simple reflective practices, like journaling or engaging in meaningful conversations with trusted friends, that we begin to excavate these buried treasures.

Within my own spiritual practice, I have found journaling to be a powerful way to reach into my well. Writing allows me to articulate my thoughts and frustrations, to hold space for my doubts while simultaneously acknowledging the moments of trust that have fortified my faith. There is a particular comfort found in knowing I can bring my worries to light, exposing them to the grace of God. Through these pages, I have often discovered insights that shift my understanding and strengthen my reliance on divine truth.

In times of spiritual drought, it is easy to feel disconnected from this source. A paralyzing feeling of separation can settle in, whispering lies that we are alone in our struggles. However, the act of reflection draws us back to that well of trust. It is crucial that we allow ourselves to engage with our emotions honestly, creating space for God to fill us up with love and understanding.

Moreover, the barriers to accessing our wells are not always born from internal struggle. External circumstances, such as life transitions, stressful events, or relationship challenges, can also impede our ability to draw from the well. The chaos of modern living can create a whirlwind that distracts us from seeking the comfort of faith.

During the pandemic, I recall how many struggled to maintain their connection with God. A friend of mine shared that she felt her well was nearly dry, a stark contrast to the vibrant faith she had carried before. It was through creative approaches—such as joining virtual prayer groups and engaging in community dialogues—that she began rediscovering her well. This illustrates that, while the approach may change, the essence of returning remains the same. Seeking out community helps us not only draw sustenance from one another but also reignite the flames of our faith.

As we turn to our wells, we must keep in mind the cyclical nature of trust. Our wells may ebb and flow, at times overflowing with enthusiasm and at others appearing bleak. This ebbing can bring feelings of inadequacy, leading us to question whether we can ever fully rely on our faith. Yet, it is essential to understand that this is part of the journey. Trust is not a destination; it is a daily choice to seek, embrace, and cultivate that connection with God.

Reflective practice can also bring to light the layers of trust we build as we progress through life. By asking ourselves questions like, "What brings me back to the well?" or "How can I ensure my well remains filled?" we can explore our reservoirs productively. These reflections shape our understanding of the well's significance in our lives.

Additionally, moments of gratitude play an essential role in cultivating our wells. Each act of recognizing gratitude serves as a drop of water rejuvenating our wells. By intentionally looking for blessings, such as a kind word from a friend, a moment of clarity in prayer, or the beauty of nature, we can begin to see our well flourish. This practice invites us to celebrate the small victories and recognize how each contributes to our trust journey.

A story that embodies this principle comes from the Devotional Guide. A family shared their journey as they navigated a tumultuous year filled with loss. Instead of allowing despair to engulf them, they attuned themselves to gratitude, seeking moments of light amidst darkness. They started a daily ritual of gathering together in the evening to share one positive experience from that day. This practice transformed their outlook, building a well of trust from which they could draw strength.

As they cultivated this habit, they began to see their well burgeon with nourishments of faith. Each shared experience acted like a pebble thrown into the well, rippling out with the recognition of God's presence in their lives. Their story stands as a reminder that the well of trust is not merely a solitary source; it is enriched when shared and celebrated within the bounds of community and togetherness.

In light of these reflections, it is essential to encourage readers to examine their own wells of trust. What lies within? Is it vibrant with faith, or does it feel stagnant? Are there barriers that may prevent access? Engaging in this reflection can be a profound endeavor, leading individuals toward greater self-awareness and spiritual growth.

Creating personal rituals is one way to cultivate a thriving well. Whether it is dedicated time for prayer, meditation, or quiet reflection in nature, these moments act as pathways to opening the well's lid, allowing the waters of trust to flow freely. Engaging in acts of service, maintaining gratitude practices, and spending time with community can all contribute to filling our wells, reminding us of the importance of interconnectedness in faith.

Reflective questions for readers to consider might include:

- When was the last time I felt a deep sense of trust in God?

- What led me to that moment?

- Are there particular fears or doubts that block my ability to draw from my well of trust? How can I confront them?

- well?
- How can I cultivate a practice of gratitude that reinforces my
- In what ways can I inspire others to engage with their wells in a meaningful way?

These questions invite readers to dig deeper into their spiritual journeys, empowering them to cultivate their wells intentionally.

As we navigate the complexities of life, our wells must serve as a sanctuary of trust, a source of spiritual nourishment. The well is a dynamic metaphor that invites us to explore the depths of our faith. It implores us to recognize the cyclical nature of trust—where we draw from it, refill it, and share it with others.

Let us not shy away from drawing near to our wells. Instead, may we remember that trusting in God is not merely a momentary act; it is a lifelong journey that beckons us to refresh our spirits, gather strength, and embrace the unveiling beauty of faith. Just as the well knows no bounds, neither does God's love for us. Together, let us cultivate our wells with intention, ensuring they remain a source of sustenance in our journeys of trust.

The Ripple Effect of Trust

Trust is a delicate yet powerful force that shapes our relationships and communities. It acts as the glue that binds individuals together, fostering connections that can withstand the tests of time and trial. In a world where uncertainty often looms, cultivating trust among friends, family, and faith communities becomes imperative, not only for personal fulfillment but also for the collective strength of the group. The stories shared here will illuminate how trust can ripple through a community, transforming individual lives and ultimately creating a more resilient and unified body of believers.

The Encourager, a key figure in our narrative, embodies the very essence of mutual support and trust. With years of experience in various faith communities, they have witnessed the transformative power of trust firsthand. Their journey illustrates how trust flourishes in environments that prioritize openness, vulnerability, and genuine connections. The Encourager shares that the initial seed of trust often begins with one person choosing to be reliable, authentic, and transparent. For them, it started in a small Bible study group, where members committed to supporting one another.

In this group, trust was cultivated through shared vulnerability. One evening, as the group gathered for their weekly meeting, the Encourager noticed that Anna, a typically cheerful member, seemed withdrawn. Sensing a shift in the atmosphere, the Encourager gently asked Anna if she wanted to share what was on her mind. Hesitation filled the room, but Anna took a deep breath and opened up about her struggles with anxiety and feelings of isolation. As she spoke, members of the group leaned in, offering empathy and understanding without judgment.

In that moment, trust rippled outward. Anna's honesty encouraged others to share their own struggles. One by one, members began to express their fears, insecurities, and challenges, creating a space of mutual support. The Encourager recalls how this vulnerability transformed the group dynamic. No longer were they merely acquaintances meeting weekly for a study; they became a community grounded in trust and authenticity.

The ripple effects were profound. As trust flourished within the group, so did their faith. Members began to pray more fervently for one another, share scripture that spoke to their struggles, and extend acts of kindness outside of their meetings. This collective faith became a lifeline for each person involved, demonstrating that they were not alone in their trials. As Anna later expressed, "I realized that trusting my peers wasn't just about sharing my burdens; it was about allowing them to carry a piece of my load."

The Encourager's experience at the Bible study group illustrates the significance of trust within faith communities. It highlights how openness leads to shared responsibility and collective growth. Mutual trust motivates community members to hold one another accountable, serve one another, and offer support during challenging times. This is not merely an abstract concept; rather, it is a tangible reality that can be seen in moments of crisis.

Take, for instance, a local church faced with the devastating news of a member's prolonged illness. The community rallied together, demonstrating trust in their relationships and commitment to one another. Members volunteered to deliver meals, provide transportation, and lend an ear for listening. The ripple effect of trust allowed the congregation to move beyond mere sympathy to active support. It's important to note that such actions were born from the foundation of trust established long before the illness emerged. When one member was vulnerable about their challenges, it opened the floodgates for others to step forward in solidarity.

An example that echoes the ripple effect of trust can be seen in a community outreach program initiated by a church. The Encourager helped lead a project aimed at serving the homeless population in their city. Trust, again, was the catalyst that propelled this initiative forward. It began with a small group of volunteers who shared a vision of making a difference. As they planned their outreach, members communicated openly about their individual strengths, struggles, and resources.

The collective trust allowed them to divvy up responsibilities according to their abilities, creating a well-rounded team. With each meeting, the Encourager noticed the way trust enhanced their planning process. Ideas flowed freely, and group members felt empowered to voice their opinions and suggestions. One volunteer even brought forth the idea of organizing a winter coat drive, spurred by their own story of needing assistance during a cold season years prior. That story of personal need resonated with the group, strengthening their resolve to support the project, and ultimately resulting in an overwhelmingly successful coat drive.

During the outreach event itself, the volunteers witnessed the powerful ramifications of their trust. As they distributed coats and offered hot meals, conversations sparked between the volunteers and those they were serving. There was a sense of camaraderie, an unspoken understanding that both parties were vulnerable and human. The volunteers learned to trust the hearts of those in need, while those receiving assistance began to trust that the volunteers genuinely cared for their well-being.

This reciprocal trust was empowering. The Encourager observed firsthand how many of those they served began to find hope amid the struggle. They saw transformational moments occur when trust broke down barriers. One recipient, a young woman named Lisa, shared how she had long felt invisible to the world. Yet, in that moment, receiving a coat from someone who expressed care and empathy, she felt seen for the first time. That feeling of being valued sparked a shift in her life, leading her to engage in the local community more actively. She began volunteering at the church and even started attending services regularly. Trust had catalyzed a change that rippled well beyond that single event.

In nurturing trust, the Encourager found that the community began embracing the idea of "faith in action." As relationships deepened, church members began to form a stronger identity as a family dedicated to living out their faith through acts of service. This dynamic created a safe haven where everyone could engage authentically without the fear of judgement. Such an environment encourages individuals to make themselves known and allows their stories to shape the community. It became no surprise then that many members began to refer to the church as their "second home," reflecting the sense of belonging that comes from deep trust.

The ripple effect extends beyond local contexts into more extensive networks of faith-based initiatives. When trust fills communities, it often leads to collaborations among multiple congregations or organizations unified by a mission. The Encourager recalls a time when several local churches came together to address the escalating issue of homelessness in their city, fueled by the foundational trust established within their individual communities. They buried their doctrinal differences in favor of collective action, which showcased the profound capacity of trust to unite disparate groups.

This collaboration allowed them to pool resources, share expertise, and expand their reach. Similarly, their unity served as a testament to their faith, illustrating how trust could overcome barriers and divisions. As they worked together, they began to generate a sense of hope for the homeless, showing these vulnerable individuals that they were not alone—each small act of care and compassion echoed within them, igniting their faith and trust in the community too.

At the heart of trust lies the issue of authenticity. The Encourager believes that genuine relationships can only be cultivated when individuals are willing to show their true selves—their joys, sorrows, and struggles. Trust is often shattered by façades or pretense. Conversely, when community members exhibit vulnerability, it empowers others to open up too.

The Encourager recalls one church event where they chose to shift the routine by allowing time for individuals to share personal testimonies in small groups. Initially, there was hesitance; fear of judgment loomed large. However, as the first person opened up about their battle with depression, a profound shift occurred. Each person who shared thereafter contributed to an atmosphere of authenticity—one that welcomed imperfections and struggles. By embracing vulnerability, they carved out a sacred space where trust emerged naturally.

This openness served as the fuel that reignited the spiritual flames within the community. People who previously held back on their faith journey saw the testimonies of those who had traversed similar paths. It encouraged them to pick up their spiritual tools again and engage with God. The ripple effect of trust meant that those who were once hesitant to share found strength in their vulnerability, which inspired others to do the same.

The Encourager concludes that trust within communities is not simply about the individuals involved; it is about understanding how interconnected their journeys truly are. When one person thrives, the benefits extend toward the collective. This principle is evident in prayer chains, where one person's request is lifted to the divine, and others join in collectively. Each prayer represents not just an individual cry for help, but a tapestry of shared faith—an assurance that no one is alone in their struggles.

As readers reflect on their journeys, they are invited to ask themselves: "Where can I cultivate trust in my community?" Perhaps it begins with vulnerability; sharing your story with a friend or gathering your community for open discussions about faith challenges. Trust begets trust, and in raising our voices, we extend the invitation for others to do the same.

Engagement matters. As participants in their own communities, readers can find ways to foster bonds of trust, whether through service, support, or simply being present for one another. The ripple effect of trust is equative to an ever-expanding circle—starting small, where each act of faith and support reverberates outward, creating waves of transformational change.

Consequently, as communities embrace trust, they breed resilience against the world's uncertainties. Each ripple becomes a testimony of God's love and presence. It becomes an affirmation that collectively, struggles can be faced, hopes can be ignited, and faith can thrive under the nurturing of trust.

In reflecting on the experiences of the Encourager and countless others within faith communities, it becomes evident that the power of trust extends beyond the individual. It flourishes through shared experiences, collective vulnerabilities, and mutual support, revealing the profound capacity for love and encouragement in every interaction. In this weave of interconnected lives, one truth becomes abundantly clear: Trust is not merely a personal endeavor; it is the thread that binds individuals into a tapestry of faith, fellowship, and family—a ripple effect that contributes enduringly to the life of the Church and the world beyond.

Embracing Uncertainty

The Unknown Path

The air was thick with uncertainty, hanging like a dense fog that crept into every corner of the Skeptic's heart. He stood at a crossroads in his life, the ground beneath his feet feeling both familiar and foreign, each step marked by the weight of doubt that settled like a shroud. The unpredictable nature of his circumstances loomed large — a shaky job, strained relationships, and questions about his faith that formed a chaotic chorus in his mind.

He often felt like he was wandering in a wilderness with no clear path. The journey ahead was obscured, overshadowed by fear and anxiety. At times, he could almost hear the voice of doubt whispering, casting shadows over his heart. "What if you make the wrong choice? What if trusting God leads you to ruin?" These thoughts taunted him, tugging at the edges of his faith, causing him to grapple with the very fabric of his beliefs.

In a moment of inner turmoil, the Skeptic recalled a familiar passage from Proverbs 3:5-6 — "Trust in the Lord with all your heart and lean not on your own understanding; in all your ways acknowledge Him, and He will make your paths straight." The words echoed in his mind, stirring a faint glimmer of hope amid the chaos. Yet, they also ignited a conflict; how could he trust in something he couldn't see? Leaning on faith felt like standing on the edge of a steep cliff, peering into an abyss where clarity escaped him.

During those sleepless nights, when uncertainties gnawed at him like a persistent ache, he often turned to stories from his faith community. He found comfort in the testimonies of others — tales of triumph over doubt, moments of surrender, and the richness of spiritual growth that blossomed from embracing the unknown.

One story, in particular, stood out. It was from a friend who had faced a life-altering diagnosis. Faced with the bleakness of their situation and the uncertainty of tomorrow, they had clung fiercely to their faith, finding strength in vulnerability. It was as if faith illuminated their path, allowing them to navigate through the murky waters of fear.

The Skeptic's reverie was interrupted by his own questions. How could he harness such unwavering faith? What would it take to embrace uncertainty as the foundation for growth, rather than as a barrier? He felt an introspective pull to explore these questions further, to confront his fears rather than flee from them.

As he began to reflect on his own uncertainties, he recognized a pattern. Each situation that had sparked trepidation in his heart had also presented opportunities for deepening his relationship with God. During layoff seasons at work, he'd experienced an unexpected support network among fellow believers, showing him firsthand the beauty of community. With job searches that felt fruitless, he often found solace in prayer, learning to rely more heavily on God as he sought clarity. In every troubling moment of uncertainty, he could trace the divine hand weaving light into his darkness.

The Skeptic's journey is not unique; countless believers have grappled with the heartache and confusion that can accompany life's unpredictable twists. The Bible is full of stories that echo this struggle, reflecting how God often calls His people into the unknown. One such example is Abraham, who stepped out in faith, not knowing where he was headed. Genesis 12:1-4 recites the power of God's call — "Go from your country, your people, and your father's household to the land I will show you." Abraham's journey began with a leap into the unseen, and he became known as the father of faith, not because he was free of doubts, but because he learned to lean into God's promises despite them.

The Skeptic longed for that same sense of purpose, a conviction that in the unknown, God was present and active. To learn from these narratives would require an honest examination of his own hesitations. So, he began to jot down the uncertainties he faced, tracing the tangled threads to their sources.

Was it fear of loss? Perhaps it was the dread of failure, or maybe the prospect of change. Whichever it was, he realized that these fears often acted as barriers to experiencing God's fullness in his life. There was an intrinsic bravery in acknowledging doubt, in confronting the very concerns that stifled his faith. As he unpacked his feelings, the words of 1 Peter 5:7 resonated deeper than ever — "Cast all your anxiety on Him because He cares for you."

The invitation to let go of burdens and uncertainties was liberating. The Skeptic breathed life into the notion of casting his worries upon God. He committed to approaching prayer as a conversation, a vulnerable space where he could lay his fears bare. If he wanted to embrace the unknown Path, it began with surrender

— a relinquishing of control and a conscious choice to trust in God's plan, regardless of its uncharted nature.

In the following weeks, the Skeptic sought to put this into practice. He took uncertain moments — particularly the looming job stability issue — and instead of succumbing to fear, he leaned into the uncertainty with prayers of affirmation. "God, I am uncertain, but I trust You. Guide me in this unknown." Each day, he found it was not a diminishing of concern but, rather, a reminder that he did not need to navigate this alone. Embracing uncertainty became a daily exercise in faith.

One evening, as he left a meeting with his fellow church group, the Skeptic was approached by a member who had been silently struggling. The weight of their shared uncertainties brought them closer, allowing hearts to intertwine as they acknowledged their individual battles. In that moment, the Skeptic recognized the ripple effect of embracing uncertainty; it fostered connection among believers who sought to uplift and support one another amidst life's unpredictability.

Life is a series of unknowns, punctuated by moments of clarity and direction given by God, but growth often occurs not in certainty but uncertainty. The Skeptic found peace and purpose in allowing himself to be a vessel through which others could witness the embracing of doubt. What he once perceived as a personal struggle became a communal opportunity, igniting sparks of encouragement within his circle.

Through narratives like his friend's story, Abraham's legacy, and his own reflections in the presence of God, the Skeptic began to see uncertainty not just as a burden to bear, but as a sacred invitation to explore the depths of trust and faith. He noted how God worked through uncertainty to unveil the intricate paths meant to be discovered, leading to spiritual maturity and greater intimacy with Him.

Inviting readers into this space, the Skeptic understood that confronting one's doubt does not mean dismissing it; instead, it requires acknowledging its presence. Readers are encouraged to reflect honestly on their own paths, recognizing that at the core of uncertainty is the potential for growth. Here are some actionable steps to bolster this journey:

1. **Identify your uncertainties**: Take time to write down the areas of your life where uncertainty stirs anxiety. Reflecting on these can reveal patterns, fears, and deep-rooted concerns.

2. **Engage with scripture**: Use Biblical narratives to remind yourself of God's constancy amid change. Passages such as Isaiah 41:10 can serve as affirmations: "So do not

fear, for I am with you; do not be dismayed, for I am your God."

3. **Seek community**: Lean into conversations with trusted friends or family. Share your uncertainties and invite them to share their own. Remember that you are not alone, and community can become a powerful source of encouragement and strength.

4. **Practice surrender through prayer**: Create the habit of prayer focused on surrender. Journal your concerns, but also write out words of trust, asking God to guide your heart through the uncertainty.

5. **Embrace vulnerability**: Be open about your battles, whether in community groups or with family. Vulnerability invites others to share in your journey and can cultivate deepen connections of trust.

6. **Look for growth opportunities**: Challenge yourself to step outside your comfort zone when faced with uncertainty. Faith often thrives in action; allow yourself to take small, courageous steps even when the end result is unclear.

7. **Reflect regularly**: Set aside time each week to reflect on experiences where you felt uncertainty and how you relied on God. Acknowledge the growth experienced during these times and celebrate the faith journey.

The Skeptic's exploration turned into a personal mission — to help others navigate the unknown paths of their lives with courage and grace. The road was bound to remain uneven; in fact, he anticipated that, just as with all journeys, new hills of uncertainty would arise. But with a heart anchored in faith and an openness to embrace all that lay ahead, he started to view uncertainty not as a roadblock, but as a vital piece of the journey.

And so, with each step into the unknown, the Skeptic took a deep breath, whispering a silent prayer. An assurance hung in the air — that with God as his guide, he could trust beyond understanding, and step boldly into the unfolding mystery of life. Embracing uncertainty became his sanctuary, an act of worship, and a reminder of the faithful presence always at his side.

Lessons from Nature

There is an ancient rhythm to existence—a dance of life that gracefully unfolds through the changing seasons. As nature transitions from the bright blooms of spring to the deep dormancy of winter, it teaches us profound lessons about uncertainty and change. Each season embodies a unique story filled with both difficulties and beauty. In this subchapter, we will delve into these lessons, drawing upon the marvelous, unpredictable world around us, and reflecting on how God's hand can be seen throughout our lives amid uncertainty.

As I stand in my backyard, the crisp air of autumn wraps around me like a cozy blanket, filling my lungs with a scent that is both invigorating and nostalgic. Leaves, dressed in hues of gold and crimson, dance playfully to the ground, whispering secrets of change. The vibrant colors are a reminder of life's cycle, each leaf a testament to beauty embraced despite the inevitability of falling away. It strikes me that nature's unpredictable shifts mirror our own life's uncertainties—the moments when we feel like we are losing parts of ourselves while being invited to grow into something new.

Spring brings with it a promise of rebirth, a reminder that even after the bleakest winter, life can renew itself. Nature exemplifies this beautifully. Trees return to life, their buds swelling with the promise of new leaves. Flowers push through the thawing earth, defying the remnants of frost. In this season, we see the shadows of uncertainty as opportunities for transformation. Within the soil, unseen roots are growing, gathering strength and nutrients while awaiting their time to bloom. This unseen work reminds us that, just like our struggles and periods of uncertainty, growth sometimes occurs without our immediate recognition.

Consider the life cycle of a seed. When planted, it plunges into darkness, enveloped in damp soil where it cannot see the sunlight or experience the world above. For a time, it remains hidden, and in that seemingly stagnant phase, it undergoes a profound transformation. The seed cracks open, and roots reach down into the darkness while a shoot stretches upward toward the light. This dynamic serves as a powerful metaphor for our lives. In moments of uncertainty and trial, we may feel buried under life's hardships, but God is often working beneath the surface, cultivating within us the strength necessary for our own transformation.

The Encourager often finds solace in nature, retreating to quiet spaces where the wilderness can speak to her. During one of her reflective walks, she stumbled across a beautiful grove of cherry blossom trees in full bloom, their petals scattered like confetti in the air. The sight was breathtaking, an explosion of joy in the midst of uncertainty. These blossoms, so ephemeral and delicate, perfectly illustrate the transient nature of life. Each spring, they bloom, but quickly fade, making their beauty all the more precious. It is in this beauty that she draws strength, understanding that life is both fleeting and beautiful, and that every moment, joyous or painful, is a gift from God.

In the stillness of her walks, she often reflects on how nature's unpredictability mimics the uncertainty of life. Each season comes with its own set of challenges: the heavy snows of winter can bury the garden, causing despair and a longing for spring. Similarly, the harsh trials we face can feel heavy and imprisoning. Yet, invariably, spring arrives, washing away the cold and revealing a panorama of life that had been silently preparing beneath the surface. God's artistry can be seen in these transitions, reminding her that no winter lasts forever.

The contrasting beauty of seasons serves as a metaphor for embracing uncertainty. Just as summer joyfully blossoms into autumn's decay, we must learn to embrace our own transitions. With God, we can find peace amid the chaos and uncertainty. Each season of our lives, be it a season of bounty or barrenness, is a chapter written into the grand narrative that God has for each of us. There is comfort in knowing that God reigns over both the sunny days and the stormy nights, and just as surely as the seasons transition, so too will our struggles give way to hope and joy.

During one particular visit to a nearby lake, the Encourager observed how the water reflected the sky, mirroring its beauty and turmoil alike. On a calm day, the surface was still, and one could see the vibrant colors of dusk reflected perfectly. But on a day marked by storms, the waters churned violently, distorting every image. This observation led her to conclude that our lives, too, will often reflect the environment we find ourselves in—moments of stillness mixed with unpredictable storms. However, beneath the surface, the life of the lake continues steadily, true to its nature, harboring fish and life unseen. So often, we may feel like the turbulent waters on the surface, but if we trust in God, we remain anchored beneath the chaos.

She recalls a time in her life when everything felt uncertain; the waters of her existence were churning. The loss of a loved one left her feeling adrift, unable to navigate through the grief and pain. With each passing day, the uncertainty weighed heavily, but it was during this time of seeking solace in nature that she discovered a symphony of hope. As she immersed herself in the stillness of the lake, she was reminded that it is okay to float through uncertainty. God, like the steady waters beneath the stormy surface, remains present, offering strength and support in times of unrest.

Nature's unpredictability can also be seen in the wildflowers that bloom in unexpected places. They often sprout through cracks in barren rocks or along forgotten paths, defying the odds stacked against them. The Encourager learned that there is beauty and grace even amidst adversity. Each wildflower's resilience serves as a powerful reminder that hope can flourish even in the least likely environments. So too can faith bloom within us, no matter how desperate and arduous our circumstances might be.

In embracing the uncertainty of life, we are encouraged to take intentional moments outdoors. Nature invites us into a shared experience of wonder and tranquility that can help us disarm the worries that plague our minds. When we spend time in God's creation, observing the small details and intricate processes, we are reminded of the delicate intricacies of our own lives. Each tree, flower, and stream speaks of God's grandeur and artistry, extending an invitation to us.

Reflecting amid nature not only connects us to our surroundings but also encourages us to carve out stillness and presence within our hectic lives. As the Encourager often journals by the babbling brook behind her home, she finds clarity and focus. The gentle sound of water flowing over stones compels her to slow down and reflect on her thoughts and prayers. In these sacred moments, the unpredictability of life transforms into a canvas of possibility. Nature teaches her that uncertainty offers space for creativity, growth, and unexpected blessings.

During one of her outdoor reflections, the Encourager noticed a caterpillar inching its way along a branch. Fascinated, she watched as it diligently worked to reach its destination. What struck her was the realization of what that caterpillar was destined to become. It wasn't merely crawling; it was on a journey of transformation to become a butterfly. In that moment, she recognized our own journeys often mirror this metamorphosis. We, too, inch along through life's uncertainties, not recognizing the greatness that God has planned for us.

Every change we encounter can feel daunting and sluggish, evoking feelings of impatience and doubt. However, just as the caterpillar eventually encloses itself within a chrysalis, we must learn to embrace transitional phases with trust—trust that there is beauty on the other side of our uncertainty. The struggle itself can foster resilience, preparing us for a glorious new beginning.

As you stand before nature, I encourage you to reflect on your surroundings, letting the beauty layer your heart with God's promises. In these still moments, ask yourself: What are the uncertainties in my life that I can surrender to God? Just as the flowers bloom after the rain, we can gather strength by acknowledging uncertainties and inviting God to blossom hope and faith within us.

Consider the rhythm of the seasons—winter, spring, summer, fall—each possessing its own beauty and fragility. When we embrace the seasons of our own lives, we can cultivate an attitude of acceptance and gratitude for what is to come. Much like the trees that will shed their leaves, we too can let go—the act of surrendering can lead to renewal.

Throughout history, countless people have found peace and strength through their journeys in nature. Many have sought out solitude among the trees, the mountains, or the waters to begin conversations with God. As the Encourager walks along nature trails, she gathers inspiration from the stories told through the landscapes. Nature, with its unpredictability and raw beauty, invites believers into communion with the Creator.

Engage your spirit with the outdoors, allowing yourself to breathe in the moments of God's artistry. Bring a notebook with you, and reflect on your journey. What parallels can you find in nature's cycles that may resonate with your own faith journey? Write freely, immersing yourself in the words God lays upon your heart.

In one of her reflective moments, the Encourager sat at a park filled with maple trees swaying gently in the breeze. Inspired by their graceful movements, she sketched images of their stunning branches and vivid leaves in her journal. As she immersed herself in the art of observation, she formed a deeper understanding that even the trees face storms, yet they stand with unyielding strength.

God allows the winds to blow and the seasons to change, but we can trust that through all, He remains a constant and unfailing presence.

With the fading sunlight casting a golden glow, she marveled at how often people overlook the beauty around them—the delicate unfolding of petals, the intricate design of spider webs glistening with dew. Just as soon as we recognize the divine fingerprints in nature, we may also acknowledge them in our own lives. Each intricate detail serves as a reminder that God is intentional in every season—whether joyful or difficult.

Allow the lessons of nature to resonate within you as you embark on your personal exploration. In the assurance that God is always at work, you can release the control that uncertainty tries to hold over your spirit. By recognizing the cycle of seasons and embracing the changes, you can actively choose to trust. Amidst the unpredictability that life will invariably present, become a witness to God's handiwork and transformational grace. Embrace the beauty of perpetual change, understanding that your journey, too, has the potential for flourishing.

May nature become our teacher, helping us find calm in the chaos and peace in our uncertainties. Embrace the seasons, the cycles of life, and the rhythms of creation. In every rustle of leaves and every whisper of wind, listen for God's voice reassuring you that amidst the unpredictability of life, He has a plan for you, uniquely crafted for growth and renewal through the ever-changing tapestry of existence. As you connect more deeply with the rhythms of nature, remember that each moment of uncertainty presents the greatest opportunity for transformation.

Find solace outdoors, and celebrate the beauty of change, understanding that every season speaks of deep trust in God's divine timing and purpose. As you reflect, may you write your story—together with all of nature's unpredictable lessons—and witness how faith leads you onward into uncharted territories filled with boundless life and love.

Faith Amidst Chaos

In times of chaos, faith can seem like a distant memory, overshadowed by the tumult of uncertainty that surrounds us. The storms that life throws our way can shake even the strongest foundations, leaving us feeling disoriented and alone. Yet, amidst the tumult, faith has a unique ability to act as a lighthouse, guiding us through the darkest nights. This subchapter delves into the stories of several characters who found themselves in chaotic situations, illustrating how they preserved their trust in God despite the overwhelming circumstances. Their journeys will serve as beacons of hope for readers, encouraging them to nurture their faith when the storms of life rage.

Consider the story of the Woman at the Well. For her, chaos was not just a fleeting moment; it was a recurring state of existence. She navigated societal rejection, personal shame, and an inner turmoil that left her feeling isolated and unworthy. On a typical day, she would fetch water during the heat of midday—the hot sun mirrored the heat of her struggles. It was in this haze of chaos, marked by her fears and doubts, that she encountered Jesus, who challenged her to confront the disarray in her life. In that pivotal moment, she had a choice: to cling to her chaos or to trust in the transformative power of faith.

When she first engaged with Jesus, her heart teetered between skepticism and the possibility of redemption. Each question posed to her was like a wave crashing against her resolve, threatening to drown her in self-doubt. Yet, amidst the chaos of her thoughts, she chose to lean into the conversation, to open her heart to the One who offered her living water. That day, she learned that faith does not mean the absence of chaos but rather the assurance that God walks with us through it.

Consider this: what storms are raging in your life right now? Perhaps it's a job loss that has you spiraling into uncertainty, a relationship fracture that leaves you feeling vulnerable, or even an unexpected health crisis that has turned your world upside down. No matter how the chaos manifests, maintaining faith amidst these storms requires intentional practice. The first step is acknowledging the chaos without allowing it to define you.

The Skeptic's journey offers another poignant example of navigating chaos through faith. He often wrestled with doubt, particularly during tumultuous moments. When faced with health issues in his family, he found himself questioning everything he believed. Instead of running from his chaos, he confronted it head-on. In those quiet moments of desperation, he turned to God not with accusations, but with raw honesty. The Skeptic kept a journal, pouring out his fears and wrestling with prayers that felt unanswered. Within those pages, he documented the tension between his hopes and his fears, allowing him to articulate the chaos that churned within.

Through his experience, it became clear that writing could serve as an effective tool during chaotic times. Journaling invites individuals to express the unfiltered thoughts that often crowd their minds during storms. It creates a space for reflection, where one can document the chaos and search for clarity. Exercise your pen the next time a storm seems to threaten your peace. Write down your fears, your prayers, and even your questions. Each word on the page becomes a declaration of your desire for understanding and your yearning for connection with God.

As we weave through this exploration of faith amidst chaos, consider the role of community in navigating turbulent waters. The Narrative of the Encourager showcases the power of fellowship during distress. When the chaos of life brought about unexpected circumstances—a job layoff that jeopardized financial stability and a family emergency that strained emotional resources—the Encourager found strength in their community. During these chaotic moments, their faith was amplified by the support of others who journeyed alongside them.

The Encourager learned the value of vulnerability when facing chaos. Instead of retreating inward, they shared their struggles with fellow believers. These conversations acted as lifelines, pulling them out of despair and reminding them of God's promises. In shared vulnerability, they discovered that others had experienced similar storms and had also clung to faith in their darkest hours. This connection transformed chaos from an isolating experience into one of communal support.

Practical exercises can help readers cultivate their faith community during chaotic times:

Establish a Prayer Circle: Gather a group of friends or family members who are willing to support each other through prayer. Schedule regular times to meet, either in person or virtually, to share concerns and pray for one another. Make this commitment a safe haven where chaos can be laid bare before God collectively.

1. **Share Stories of Hope**: Encourage group members to

share stories of how faith has guided them through their own chaotic moments. Each testimony can serve as an encouraging reminder that faith isn't an isolated experience but a shared journey woven together by the threads of God's goodness.

2. **Create a Chaos Journal Group**: Similar to a book club but focused on chaos, invite friends to keep journals during particularly hectic times. At appointed meetings, share excerpts from your journals. This could serve as a powerful way to illustrate the oscillation between chaos and faith, giving voice to fears while also highlighting moments of hope.

The journey through chaos is inherently personal and often riddled with questions that remain unanswered. Yet, there's a profound strength in recognizing that others too are navigating their own storms. In acknowledging the shared experience of chaos and faith, we can find a sense of belonging.

Turning back to the Woman at the Well, her story is also a testament to resilience—a quality that flourishes in the face of uncertainty. After her encounter with Jesus, she transformed from an outcast to a fearless evangelist, sharing her testimony with her entire town. Her internal chaos began to subside as she found purpose amidst her tumult. By trusting in what Jesus offered her, she stepped boldly into her new identity and mission.

When we embrace chaos alongside faith, we begin to discover the avenues where we grow. Faith can flourish in the most unexpected places. Through intentional reflection and action during the storm, we can carve out moments of peace. The Skeptic's experience highlights the beauty of accepting doubt as part of faith. He learned that chaos could be layered with meaning and growth; it signals transition and an invitation for God to work in ways that may not align with our expectations.

As you ponder your own moments of chaos, remember that these times can lead to profound transformation. When fear threatens to overtake you, remind yourself of the faith stories that have preceded yours. What might God be preparing in you during these challenging moments?

Life's storms often challenge our understanding of what our faith can endure. In chaos, faith may seem more fragile than ever; however, it is the very chaos that can reveal the depth of your trust. To navigate these tumultuous waters, readers can lean into exercises that support their spiritual journeys:

1. **Meditation on Scripture**: Select meaningful verses that anchor your faith in turbulent times. During a chaotic moment, meditate on these scriptures. Allow their truths to penetrate your heart and fill you with peace. One practical exercise involves writing down your chosen scriptures and carrying them with you. When chaos arises, take a moment to read them, let them wash over you, and remind yourself of God's presence.

2. **Practice Gratitude Amidst Chaos**: Even in the storm, there is always something to be grateful for. Start a gratitude list during difficult times. Each day, write down three things for which you are grateful, no matter how small. This practice can shift your focus from fear to appreciation, enabling you to see God's hand at work even in chaotic circumstances.

3. **Engage in Servant Leadership**: When faced with chaos, consider ways to serve others within your community. Acts of kindness can alter the narrative of fear, placing it on a less powerful pedestal. Volunteering during chaotic times can help provide perspective and purpose, showcasing God's

love through your actions.

In maintaining faith amidst chaos, remember that you are not alone in your journey. The threads of your story are interwoven with the lives of others who have navigated similar storms. As you venture through chaos, allow the experiences of the Woman at the Well, the Skeptic, and the Encourager to guide you. Let their paths inspire your own choices to cultivate trust in God amid the chaos that life throws your way.

Lastly, let's consider the significance of reflection after the storm. The storms we navigate often leave behind lessons, blessings, and opportunities for growth. The journey does not end once the chaos subsides—rather, it transforms into something new. It's essential to take the time to reflect on what has transpired, the assurances you've gained, and how your faith has evolved.

1. **Set Aside Reflection Time**: After a chaotic experience has passed, find a quiet space to reflect. Journal about the emotional and spiritual aspects of your journey. What challenges did you face? What insights did you receive about yourself and your faith?

2. **Celebrate Resilience**: Acknowledge the strength you demonstrated during the chaos. Consider how your faith was a guiding light. Share these reflections with trusted friends, reinforcing the significance of community connection.

3. **Look Forward with Hope**: As you embrace the lessons learned from chaos, set intentions for how you will carry your faith forward. Each storm weathered can build a foundation for future challenges. Prepare yourself with the understanding that faith will anchor you through new trials, reminding you that God is ever-present amid the uncertainties of life.

Ultimately, the journey of maintaining faith amidst chaos challenges our understanding of what trust really means. It invites us to lean into the uncomfortable and to explore how faith can be a steadfast companion during our darkest moments. May these stories and exercises inspire you as you navigate your own storms. Embrace the knowledge that, even in your chaos, God walks with you, illuminating your path with unwavering love and unwavering hope.

Daily Surrender

Understanding Surrender

In the quiet moments of our lives, when the world around us spins in chaos, the concept of surrender often surfaces as a bittersweet necessity. Yet, for many, the idea of surrendering feels more like a daunting surrendering of self than a graceful act of faith. We cling to our worries, our ambitions, and our need to control outcomes, believing that by holding on tightly, we can navigate life's uncertainties. However, as illustrated through the transformative journey of the Woman at the Well, embracing daily surrender can lead to profound peace and clarity—a lesson as applicable today as it was in biblical times.

The encounter between Jesus and the Woman at the Well presents a powerful narrative of surrender that resonates deeply with anyone grappling with issues of control and anxiety. She arrives at the well, perhaps expecting a mundane task, but instead meets someone who will forever alter the trajectory of her life. Jesus engages her in a profound exchange, unveiling her past and offering her a new identity—one not rooted in shame or isolation but in deep acceptance and love.

As we read about her reluctant transformation, we begin to see the layers of her struggle with surrender. Caught in a cycle of disappointment and societal rejection, she may have been tempted to hold onto her familiar pain, believing that it defined her. Yet, through her interaction with Jesus, we witness a pivotal shift—a release of her burdens and a step toward embracing hope. This is the essence of surrender: a relinquishing of control and an act of trust in something greater than oneself.

Scripture offers us countless passages that speak to the importance of surrendering our worries to God. In Matthew

11:28-30, Jesus invites all who are weary and burdened to come to Him for rest. This invitation is a gentle reminder that we do not have to navigate our struggles alone. Each day, we face a choice: to carry the weight of our worries or to bring them to the very source of peace. Surrender, then, is not a one-time event but a daily act of relinquishing our grip on life's controls.

To guide ourselves toward this practice of daily surrender, we can engage with reflective prompts that encourage introspection. What burdens am I carrying today? What fears keep me from trusting God fully? Where am I resisting the act of surrender, and why? Such questions invite us to tap into our inner landscape, recognizing the ways we attempt to control our lives and the barriers that prevent us from yielding to God's plans.

As part of this exploration, we can look to the experiences shared in the Devotional Guide, who emphasizes the tangible benefits that come from the practice of surrender. One story that stands out involves a character who struggled with anxiety about their job. Every morning, this individual would wake with a racing heart, fearful of failure, judgment, and the unpredictability of the workplace. After attending a retreat centered on faith and surrender, they began to incorporate daily surrender into their routine. Each morning, they would take a few moments to identify their fears and hand them over to God in prayer. What began as a struggle soon transformed into a sanctuary of peace, a space where they could transition from anxiety to trust, allowing room for the divine to work.

This individual's journey illustrates that surrender often means confronting the discomfort of uncertainty; it is the realization that we may not have control over the outcomes, but we can trust the One who does. It is through these moments of yielding that we begin to see our worries diminish and our faith flourish. Each day becomes an opportunity to start anew, offering our struggles to God and experiencing His grace in return.

In addition to acknowledging personal burdens, surrendering involves an openness to God's guidance. Proverbs 3:5-6 reminds us, "Trust in the LORD with all your heart and lean not on your own understanding; in all your ways submit to him, and he will make your paths straight." Here lies the crux of daily surrender: it is not merely about letting go but about inviting God into our everyday decisions, seeking His wisdom for the road ahead. As we practice this surrender, we find that clarity becomes a companion on our journey, illuminating the path we may not yet see.

Embracing surrender also invites us to reflect on the moments when we've relinquished control and witnessed the fruition of God's promises. I recall a time when my family faced a significant crossroad—the decision to relocate for new opportunities. The weight of uncertainty hung over us, each hypothetical what-if amplifying our resistance. After much prayer and conversation, we decided to surrender our fears and trust God's direction. By engaging in regular prayer and seeking counsel from our faith community, we gradually grew more comfortable with the idea. What initially felt like an insurmountable leap of faith transformed into a series of small steps—each brimming with hope and newfound clarity. Looking back, I can see how God orchestrated the details in ways we couldn't have imagined, confirming that surrender often leads to unexpected blessings.

As we navigate our own daily surrenders, it's essential to recognize the common struggles we face. Control manifests in myriad ways—our attempts to micromanage relationships, our desire for perfectionism, or our need for certainty in the future. In each case, surrendering can feel risky and often evokes discomfort. Yet, the beauty lies in the internal transformation that occurs; it is in letting go of our grip on control that we make space for deeper faith.

Moreover, learning to lean into surrender can catalyze healing. For instance, the Woman at the Well, upon recognizing her need for Jesus, surrendered her past and the shame she carried. Her boldness to acknowledge her truth to Christ marked the beginning of healing—not only for herself but for those she would later influence within her community. Her story highlights that surrender can also empower us to become vessels of hope for others, illustrating the ripple effect of yielding our lives to God.

As we reflect on these themes of surrender, it is important to create actionable steps for incorporating this practice into our daily lives. One effective way is through the establishment of a "surrender journal." This journal serves as a safe space for writing down worries, fears, and aspirations. Each entry can begin with a short prayer inviting God to take the burdens we carry. As you fill the pages, watch for patterns that emerge—the areas where God is calling you to surrender and what insights or messages of hope arise from these moments of reflection.

Another practical step could involve setting specific 'Surrender Times' throughout the day. Perhaps during your morning coffee, you could pause to breathe deeply, focusing on placing your cares before God. Or in the evening, as you wind down, take time to reflect on what occurred throughout the day and invite God into your thoughts, surrendering any residual anxieties or unresolved feelings. By doing so, you create a tentative ritual, reinforcing that surrender is not a life-long expedition but rather a series of intentional moments we cultivate daily.

As we endeavor to embrace daily surrender, it's paramount to remain gentle with ourselves in the process. Recognizing that surrender may not come easily can alleviate the pressure of perfection. It is a practice—much like developing a muscle— requiring time and grace. Just as the Woman at the Well discovered a newfound identity in Christ, we too are on a journey, learning through our experiences how to entrust our lives to God's care.

Our faith journey is a continual unfolding, and in the act of surrender, we unearth a profound truth: that we are never alone in this process. Surrounding us are fellow believers who share in the struggle of yielding control, and through community, we can collectively support one another in our journeys. As we bond with one another in faith, we cultivate an environment that nurtures trust and allows us to surrender without fear of judgment or isolation.

Through focusing on daily surrender, we tap into a wellspring of spiritual nourishment that leads us toward deeper faith and understanding. In doing so, we not only transform our internal struggles but also cultivate a community of support, encouragement, and hope. As we examine our lives through the lens of God's promises, let us embrace the call to surrender, knowing that each moment we relinquish control is a profound step towards peace and clarity.

In closing, remember that surrendering daily to God doesn't mean leaving behind our ambitions and dreams; rather, it invites us to yield our hopes to Him, trusting that He will mold and shape our paths. Much like the Woman at the Well, we find that in surrendering our pasts and trusting God with our futures, we open ourselves to an abundance of grace—one that allows us to walk boldly into the life He has designed. Each act of surrender serves as a brushstroke, painting a portrait of faith that reflects resilience, courage, and deep connection to the divine, guiding us to embrace the beautiful journey ahead.

Practical Steps to Surrender

In a world where we often feel the weight of our responsibilities pressing down on us, the concept of surrender can appear daunting. It is easy to believe that by holding on tightly to our worries and fears, we can somehow manage the chaos of life.

Yet, the truth is that surrender is not a sign of weakness but rather an act of courageous faith. It is the intentional choice to release our burdens into the hands of a loving and capable God.

To embrace the practice of daily surrender, we can adopt practical strategies that support us in letting go—and, in turn, cultivate deeper trust in God's plan for our lives. This subchapter will highlight actionable steps, share stories of transformation, and address common obstacles that may hinder our journey toward surrender.

Creating a Surrender Journal

One of the most effective tools in the practice of daily surrender is the creation of a surrender journal. A surrender journal is a personal space where you can articulate your worries, fears, and prayers. The act of writing fosters clarity and self-expression, allowing you to examine your thoughts and emotions more fully. Here's how to start:

1. **Select Your Journal**: Choose a journal that resonates with you—something that inspires you to write. It could be a beautiful notebook, a simple spiral-bound pad, or even a digital platform if you prefer typing.

2. **Set a Regular Time**: Establish a routine for journaling. This could be in the morning, as you reflect on the day ahead, or in the evening, as you review the day's events. Consistency is key; making this a daily ritual will enhance your experience.

3. **Begin with Gratitude**: Start each entry by listing three things you are grateful for. This practice can shift your focus from worries to blessings, setting a positive tone for your writing.

4. **Articulate Your Burdens**: Write down your concerns

and fears, no matter how trivial they may seem. By putting pen to paper, you externalize your worries, which can relieve the burden you feel within. Allow yourself to be honest and vulnerable in this space.

5. **Pray Over What You've Written**: After articulating your worries, take time to pray over them. Ask God to take your burdens, to provide comfort, and to align your heart with His will. You might write prayers directly in your journal, or you can use this time for silent contemplation.

6. **Reflect on His Faithfulness**: At the end of each week or month, reflect back on your entries. Note areas where God has worked in your life, providing clarity or comfort. This practice reinforces the truth that surrender leads to trust and transformation.

The Encourager, one of our central figures, found immense relief in maintaining a surrender journal. Initially hesitant to share their deepest fears, they began writing during moments of distress, pouring their heart onto the pages. Over time, The Encourager realized that articulating their worries helped them feel less isolated. They often recall a particularly stressful season at work—a time when they felt overwhelmed with project deadlines and personal responsibilities. Writing down their fears not only lightened their burden but also opened their heart to God's peace.

As they flipped back through earlier entries, The Encourager discovered the many times God had intervened. This exercise reignited their faith and reassured them that God was present through every storm. The journal became a cherished companion in their daily walk of surrender.

Establishing a Surrender Ritual

Beyond journaling, developing a surrender ritual can serve as a tangible expression of releasing control and embracing trust. This ritual can be as simple or elaborate as you wish, depending on what resonates with your personal faith journey. Here are practical steps to put a ritual into place:

1. **Choose a Location**: Designate a peaceful spot in your home—a place where you feel calm and free to express your thoughts and emotions. It might be a cozy chair, a quiet corner in your garden, or even a local park where you feel connected to God.

2. **Gather Your Materials**: Consider including items that enhance your ritual experience. This could be a candle, a meaningful scripture card, a stone representing your burdens, or even music that soothes your spirit. Each element should invoke a sense of divine connection.

3. **Create a Quiet Space**: Begin by creating stillness around you. Take a few deep breaths, allowing your mind to settle. This peace will prepare your heart for the surrender process.

4. **Invite God into the Space**: Start your ritual by inviting God's presence. You may want to read a scripture passage that speaks to surrender, such as Psalm 55:22, "Cast your cares on the Lord and He will sustain you." This sets the tone for your time together.

5. **Visualize Surrender**: Spend a few moments visualizing what it looks like to surrender your worries to God. You might picture holding onto them tightly, then purposefully letting go, allowing them to drift into the atmosphere. Embrace the freedom that comes from releasing control.

6. **Make a Symbolic Gesture**: Conclude your ritual with a symbolic gesture. You could write your worries on a piece of paper and then tear it up or burn it safely, releasing their power.

Alternatively, you might physically place a stone in a designated spot as a symbol of the burdens you are surrendering.

7. **Close in Prayer**: End your ritual with a heartfelt prayer, expressing gratitude for God's love and reiterating your desire to trust Him completely. Ask for the strength to continue practicing surrender in your daily life.

The Encourager embraced a surrender ritual when life felt particularly chaotic. They would take time each week to retreat to their garden, lit a candle, and read passages that spoke to their heart. As they laid their burdens before God, they would visualize placing each worry into His capable hands. The ritual transformed their approach to stress, renewing their faith and reaffirming the importance of surrender. The Encourager often shares how these moments became a refuge for their soul—a time when they remembered that they were never alone in the struggle.

Identifying Obstacles to Surrender

While practicing surrender can lead to spiritual growth, various obstacles may hinder our ability to fully let go. Recognizing these barriers can help us navigate the challenges that arise. Below are common obstacles to surrender alongside strategies for overcoming them:

1. **Fear of Losing Control**: A significant barrier many face is the fear of losing control. This fear often leads individuals to hold onto their worries tightly, believing that managing them themselves is a means of protection. To overcome this, reflect on the moments in life when clinging to control brought more anxiety than peace. By recalling those instances, we can begin to understand that true safety exists in trusting God.

2. **Doubt and Uncertainty**: Doubt can breed reluctance when it comes to surrender. We may fear that surrendering

our worries will lead to profound uncertainty or, worse, a sense of abandonment. Counter this by engaging with scripture that affirms God's faithfulness (e.g., 1 Peter 5:7, "Cast all your anxiety on Him because He cares for you"). Grasping the truth that God is ever-present helps diminish fear associated with uncertainty.

3. **Belief that We Must 'Earn' God's Help**: Many individuals struggle with the notion that they must earn God's assistance through their own efforts. This belief can create a cycle of striving rather than surrendering. Consider the beautiful truth that God's love and grace are freely given. Reflecting on God's unconditional love can ease the pressure to earn His help and open our hearts to simply receiving it.

4. **Pride and Self-Sufficiency**: Pride can masquerade as self-sufficiency, convincing us that we don't need assistance. To counteract this, remind yourself of moments when you faced challenges beyond your capability. Embrace the understanding that surrender is not an admission of failure; rather, it is a display of humility and faith.

5. **Rushing the Process**: In a world that values quick results, we may rush into surrender without allowing time for reflection. Acknowledge that surrender often requires a journey of its own. Cultivate patience by creating space for slow and deliberate decisions. Surrender is not a one-time action but an ongoing practice, and it unfolds over time.

The Encourager often reflects on their own journey with these obstacles. For years, they believed that God expected them to handle everything on their own; this belief led to burnout and a long season of anxiety. When they finally learned to surrender, the experience was met with resistance, tinged by their pride and self-doubt. However, as The Encourager began to confront these obstacles through prayer and reflection, they discovered the freedom that surrendering brought to their life. God's faithfulness became evident, and they recognized that living in surrender opened the door to experiencing abundant peace.

Taking Small Steps Toward Daily Surrender

As we embark on the journey of daily surrender, it is essential to remember that small steps lead to significant transformation. Below are actionable steps to practice surrender each day:

1. **Morning Affirmations**: Begin your day with affirmations that reinforce your commitment to surrender. Phrases like "I trust you, God," or "I release my worries into your hands" can set a positive tone for the day ahead. Speak these affirmations out loud to anchor your heart in trust.

2. **Mindfulness Moments**: Throughout your day, set aside moments to practice mindfulness. Pause for a few breaths whenever you feel anxious or overwhelmed. Use these moments as reminders to invite God into the situation. A simple prayer, such as "Help me trust you in this moment," can cultivate peace.

3. **Evening Reflection**: Conclude your day with reflection on what you surrendered. Take note of situations or feelings that originally felt overwhelming yet had manageable outcomes. These reflections reinforce the power of surrender, reminding you that you can trust God with your worries.

4. **Engage in Acts of Service**: Serving others can lend perspective to our own burdens. Find opportunities to support friends, family, or community members. By taking the focus off ourselves and our worries, we can find renewed strength in surrendering to God's greater purpose.

5. **Practice Gratitude**: Cultivate a habit of gratitude by listing five things each day for which you are thankful. Recognizing God's blessings in your life makes it easier to trust Him with your concerns. Gratitude serves as a profound reminder of His goodness.

6. **Soul Connections**: Connect deeply with individuals who uplift your spirit and encourage surrender. Engage in conversations about faith, sharing both victories and struggles. Hearing stories from others can instill hope and inspire you to keep practicing surrender.

7. **Celebrate Progress**: Acknowledge your progress in surrendering. Take time to celebrate small victories and transformations. Whether it's through journaling or sharing with a friend, recognizing progress can motivate you to continue your journey of surrender.

By embracing these small steps, you set yourself up for a profound transformation in how you relate to your worries. The Encourager embodies this practice in their daily life, taking time to affirm their faith and reflect nightly on God's goodness. Each of these steps serves to build their capacity to release control, inspiring others in their community to do the same.

Conclusion

The journey of daily surrender is both a profound and rewarding experience, leading to a deeper trust in God's plans and His timing. Through practical steps like maintaining a surrender journal, establishing rituals, and tackling obstacles, we can cultivate this essential practice in our lives.

Remember, surrender is not a destination but a continual journey of faith. The Encourager's stories and experiences provide relatable insights into the importance of surrender in transforming your faith. As you begin to intentionally practice surrender through small steps, may you find the freedom, peace, and clarity that comes from releasing your burdens into the hands of a loving God who cares for you deeply. Embrace the transformation that comes with daily surrender, recognizing that with each act of letting go, you are nurturing a deeper, more profound relationship with your Creator.

The Freedom in Letting Go

As we tread the intricate path of faith, there comes a moment when we realize that true freedom lies not in our ability to control, but in our willingness to let go. Surrendering to God becomes the key that unlocks a life of liberation, allowing us to experience the emotional and spiritual lightness that accompanies trust. In this journey, we will hear the testimonies of individuals whose lives have been transformed through surrender, showcasing the profound benefits that arise when we relinquish our grasp on worries and anxieties.

Let us begin with the story of Sarah, a young mother whose life had become a whirlwind of commitments and responsibilities. Balancing her role as a caregiver with her desire for personal achievement, Sarah frequently felt overwhelmed. The pressures of work, family, and social expectations weighed heavily on her shoulders, and she found herself perpetually anxious, trying to meet the demands of every aspect of her life.

One afternoon, as Sarah sat in her living room feeling particularly burdened, she received a call from a friend inviting her to attend a church service focused on the theme of surrender. Although hesitant, she decided to go, desperate for a sense of peace. As she listened to the sermon, the pastor spoke directly to her heart, emphasizing that surrendering to God was not an act of defeat, but rather a bold declaration of trust. The pastor illustrated beautifully how letting go of our tightly held control allows God to work in ways we often cannot imagine.

That night, Sarah returned home with a new perspective. She courageously approached each worry she had been nursing with the intention of surrendering it to God. Naming her fears aloud, she began to hand them over: her anxieties about being a good mother, the looming deadlines at work, her relationships filled with tension. In each declaration, she felt an incremental lifting of the weight she had carried for so long.

"I surrender my need for perfection," she whispered one evening, sitting alone in her quiet space. "I trust that God loves me in my imperfection." With every passing day, she continued to lay down her burdens, and what she discovered was nothing short of liberating. As she embraced the act of surrender, Sarah began to witness a shift within her spirit. Each worry she released was like letting go of a balloon, watching it float away from her grasp, soaring upward towards the heavens.

By celebrating her journey of surrender each day, Sarah found herself reflecting on the emotional freedom that came with acknowledging her limitations. Gone were the days of measuring her worth by her productivity or the approval of others. In their place blossomed a renewed sense of self, rooted in an identity fortified by faith. She began to prioritize moments of stillness, engaging more deeply in prayer and meditation. It was during these times that Sarah felt God's profound presence washing over her. The burdens she had once carried became lighter, muted by a sense of peace that only God could provide.

Sarah's testimony is just one among many that rejoice in the freedom of letting go. Across ages and backgrounds, the theme of surrender resonates deeply. Take, for instance, the story of Mark, a businessman whose life was consumed by the pursuit of success. Mark was no stranger to ambition; his drive had propelled him through his career, but it also left a trail of exhaustion, anxiety, and strained relationships. Consumed by his work, he found it nearly impossible to let go of the relentless pursuit of excellence.

Eventually, Mark found himself at a crossroads. As his health began to decline due to stress, he encountered a wise mentor who encouraged him to reexamine his life. "Have you ever thought about what it means to surrender?" the mentor asked. Mark shook his head, accustomed to taking charge of every aspect of his life.

Intrigued yet skeptical, Mark began to explore this notion. He attended workshops and sought out scripture that spoke of surrendering one's life to God. Over time, the idea began to take root. He began praying earnestly, wrestling with his fears around relinquishing control over his career, finances, and relationships.

The pivotal moment came during a silent retreat. Mark set aside time to focus entirely on God, away from the demands of his everyday life. As he sat on a hillside, looking out over a beautiful valley, he felt the weight of his ambitions press heavily upon him. In that sacred moment, he lifted his hands to the sky and declared, "I surrender my need for control. I trust that You have a greater plan."

It was as if a dam had broken within him. Tears streamed down his face as the freedom of his surrender flowed in. By letting go of the constant need to strive, Mark found a new pathway to peace. His relationships improved as he became more present, his heart opened to those around him. Mark realized that success, rooted in the world's standards, paled in comparison to the freedom of surrendering his pursuits for the sake of a more meaningful life.

As Sarah and Mark share their experiences, they echo a universal truth: surrendering to God is an act steeped in trust, and it cultivates a deep emotional and spiritual benefit. Letting go of control allows us to embrace the fullness of life, marked by joy, peace, and connection.

But why do so many of us struggle with surrender? The answer often lies in the fear of the unknown. We may cling to our worries not because they serve us, but because they offer the illusion of control—the notion that if we keep our burdens close, we can somehow navigate life's unpredictable terrain.

Surrendering challenges that notion. It forces us to confront our vulnerabilities and acknowledge our limitations. In this process, God calls us to step forward in faith, to release our gripping anxieties and trust in His unfolding plan. Just like the Woman at the Well, who initially approached Jesus burdened with shame and fear, we can transform our insecurities into faith through the powerful act of letting go.

Like Sarah and Mark, each of us has the potential to experience transformation as we embrace the freedom found in surrender. As we reflect on our individual journeys, we are invited to examine what we might be holding onto that hinders our growth. What fears have we been nursing? What concerns have woven themselves into the fabric of our daily existence and stifled joy?

Let us take a moment to engage in the reflective exercise that concludes this subchapter. Find a quiet space where you can be alone with your thoughts. Grab a journal or a piece of paper to write. Close your eyes and take a few deep breaths, allowing the rhythm of your breathing to ground you in the present moment.

Begin by asking yourself: What do I need to surrender today? Is it a fear of failure? A relationship burdened by conflict? The pressure to meet expectations? Write down these thoughts, allowing them to flow freely onto the page.

Next, reflect on how these worries have impacted your life. Take a moment to consider the emotional weight they carry. How have they influenced your relationships, your peace of mind, and your connection to God? Acknowledge the toll they have taken, and honor your feelings surrounding them.

Now, shift your focus towards the promise of surrender. Write down what it might feel like to release these burdens into God's hands. Embrace the idea of freedom; imagine the lightness you could experience if you allowed yourself to let go.

Finally, conclude this exercise with a prayer of surrender. Speak to God sincerely about the concerns you have identified. Ask for His help in letting go. Surrender your fears, acknowledging that you cannot control everything and that trusting Him is the pathway to peace.

"God, I surrender my need for control. I trust You with my worries. Help me to embrace the freedom that comes from letting go. Amen."

As you finish this exercise, carry the sense of freedom with you. Remind yourself that surrender is an ongoing process, a daily practice that can lead to profound transformation. Celebrate each step, however small, towards releasing what weighs heavy on your heart.

In this journey of faith, may we all find the courage to surrender our daily worries and embrace the divine freedom that God lovingly offers. As we learn to let go, we simultaneously draw closer to Him, discovering the fullness of life that comes from trusting His plan above our own. In surrendering, we not only find liberation ourselves but also inspire others to embark on their journey of surrender, creating a ripple effect that glorifies His Kingdom.

Faith in Action

Taking Steps in Faith

Faith is an active, living force that propels us beyond the confines of our human understanding. It is a call to action, an invitation to step outside our comfort zones and enter into the realm of the extraordinary. Each day presents us with opportunities to embody our beliefs, to take tangible steps aligned with the faith that resides within us. Yet, the act of demonstrating faith can be fraught with uncertainty, hesitation, and a myriad of emotions ranging from anticipation to fear. It is through stepping out in faith that we discover the true nature of belief—not merely as a set of convictions, but as a dynamic engagement with the world around us.

Take, for instance, the story of Sarah, a woman who found herself at a crossroads in her life. Sarah had always dreamed of starting her own business, an artisan bakery that incorporated her unique flair for baking. However, life had delivered its fair share of challenges: raising children, balancing a job with family responsibilities, and dealing with the uncertainties that life often hands us. For years, Sarah buried her dreams beneath the weight of practicalities and the relentless drumbeat of doubt.

One evening, while attending a local women's retreat, Sarah listened intently as a speaker shared her journey of faith—a journey marked by both triumphs and tribulations. This woman spoke of the importance of stepping out in faith and trusting God to provide, not just in times of abundance but in the moments of scarcity and doubt. Sarah found herself captivated, her heart quickening at the thought that perhaps it was time for her to act on that longing she had kept alive within, to trust that God would provide the way.

Inspired by this declaration of faith, Sarah took a leap. She decided to host a pop-up bakery event at a nearby community center. With no prior business experience, Sarah had to confront her insecurities head-on. Would people come? What if they didn't like her baking? Could she truly handle the logistics of running a business? Yet, nestled within her fear, Sarah felt a flicker of hope igniting within her spirit. This wasn't just about baking; it was a manifestation of her desire to use her God-given talents.

Weeks passed as she prepared for her pop-up bakery, juggling her responsibilities at home while trying to figure out how to create a brand and market her products. On the day of the event, she found herself standing nervously at a beautifully decorated booth filled with her lovingly crafted pastries. As the crowd trickled in, Sarah's heart raced with a mix of hope and anxiety. To her astonishment, people began to sample her goods and share warm words of praise.

But it wasn't just the sales that filled her with joy; it was the community that formed around this simple act of faith. Customers became friends who supported her, offering encouragement as she walked through the ups and downs of her entrepreneurial journey. Throughout it all, Sarah learned that stepping out in faith brings unexpected blessings, both for oneself and for those around them. Her small bakery event not only fueled her passion; it forged connections that uplifted others.

Reflecting on Sarah's story, we find the essence of taking steps in faith—an essence that intertwines trust, courage, and the willingness to act amidst uncertainty. The importance of putting faith into action cannot be overstated. Faith that remains dormant is like seed that never sees the light of day. It requires a nurturing environment to grow, but ultimately, it needs the sun's rays and the rain's touch to ignite the transformative process of germination.

Another powerful narrative comes from Marcus, who felt a distinct call to serve in his community. A committed volunteer at a local homeless shelter, he often pondered how to make a more significant impact beyond mere service hours. His faith prompted him, urging him to seek innovative solutions to the issues faced by the individuals and families he encountered. One day, after helping a family find emergency housing, he was struck with a newfound purpose: to create a community resource center that would provide not just meals, but also job training, tutoring, and counseling.

Marcus recognized that establishing such a center would require extensive planning, funding, and collaboration with others. He felt a swell of doubt rise, yet he also felt an unmistakable call resonating in his spirit. He decided to act on that call. Marcus assembled a group of like-minded individuals, each bringing their unique expertise and passion to the table. Together, they organized fundraisers, applied for grants, and collaborated with local businesses to garner support.

The road was fraught with challenges. Several funding proposals were rejected, and at times the group felt overwhelmed by the sheer amount of work required. However, Marcus remained steadfast in his belief that they were being led by a higher purpose. Encouraging everyone to remain focused on their vision, he often reminded them of the people they served—the families who deserved more than just handouts.

The community center eventually opened its doors, a beautiful testament to what can happen when faith is put into action. It became a hub of hope and transformation, illustrating the profound impact of collective faith-driven efforts. People found jobs, individuals enrolled in classes, and families received the support they desperately needed. In this instance, the act of stepping out in faith created ripples of change that extended far beyond what Marcus initially envisioned.

It is essential to recognize that not every step taken in faith will lead to immediate success or clear outcomes. The journey is often marked with lessons that arise from failures and detours. For instance, during the early days of planning the community center, one of the proposed initiatives—a mentorship program—failed to gain traction. Instead of perceiving this as a setback, Marcus and his team used the experience to re-evaluate their approach and discover alternative paths to fulfilling their mission. By listening to feedback and remaining adaptable, they learned that setbacks can often lead to better solutions that serve the community more effectively.

The complexity of acting on belief is illuminated through these examples. Each story highlights the courage it takes to step beyond one's comfort zone, coupled with the certainty that faith isn't just a mental agreement but a call to action. Engaging with our beliefs requires an active response; it requires us to continually evaluate how we can embody those beliefs in daily life.

Insights from the Devotional Guide further underscore this theme. The author shares personal experiences of stepping out in faith in their own life, recounting a moment when they sensed a divine nudge to reach out to an estranged family member. Initially hesitant, fearing rejection, the author thought about the principles of forgiveness and love central to their faith. Summoning courage, they initiated a conversation that led to reconciliation, reminding them that faith isn't merely about belief but the tangible steps we take to live out those beliefs.

A reflective exercise after the narrative invites readers to consider their faith actions over the past year. What bold steps have they taken? Where have they felt God nudging them to act? Readers can ponder moments in their lives when they felt led to make a decision that was outside their comfort zone, exploring the emotions tied to those actions. Did they experience joy, fear, excitement, or perhaps uncertainty?

For many, incorporating faith into everyday life can begin with small, intentional steps. It might be as simple as offering kindness to a stranger or volunteering for a local charity. These acts, while seemingly small, can ignite transformation within ourselves and in others. As readers reflect on their experiences, they are encouraged to identify areas where they can take new steps, whether that's by serving in their church, reaching out to a friend in need, or initiating conversations about faith within their communities.

The journey of faith is inherently relational. How we embody our beliefs can influence not only our lives but also the lives of those around us. Consider the story of Leah, a young woman who felt a heart for her peers struggling with mental health challenges. Understanding that many people felt isolated and unheard, she was compelled to create a safe space where students could share their experiences and seek support.

Taking steps in faith, Leah organized a series of discussion groups at her school. Initially apprehensive, she put out flyers and invited her classmates to join. The response was better than she expected; soon, a diverse group of students began to gather and share their stories. For many, it was the first time they felt understood, and that sense of community began to flourish.

Yet, there were also moments of doubt and fear. Leah encountered students who were skeptical about the groups, questioning their purpose and validity. In those moments, her faith in the mission propelled her forward. She leaned on prayer, seeking guidance and wisdom to navigate these conversations, understanding that the act of faith sometimes means gently challenging the fears and misconceptions of others.

Through her determination, Leah saw lives transformed as connections were made, friendships formed, and individuals began embracing their vulnerabilities. This was more than just a support group; it became a movement of healing driven by faith in action. Leah discovered that her willingness to take a step, despite her fears, created a safe harbor that changed how her peers viewed themselves and their struggles.

As we explore the importance of putting faith into action, it's essential to acknowledge the variety of pathways that exist. Each individual has their unique story, perspective, and calling. Faith acts as a compass, guiding us toward opportunities and nudging us to step beyond the familiar. Readers are encouraged to seek within themselves the passions, talents, and opportunities that beckon them to act.

To inspire reflection, let's consider some actionable steps readers can take as they begin or continue their journey of acting on faith.

1. **Identify Your Passions**: Take some time to reflect on what truly ignites your heart. What causes do you feel passionate about? What gifts do you possess that could be used to serve others? Identifying these will help guide your steps forward.

2. **Set Allure Goals**: Think of one area in your life where you feel inclined to act on your faith. Set a small, attainable goal related to it. Whether it's volunteering at a local organization, reaching out to someone in need, or learning more about a cause, make it a tangible commitment.

3. **Engage in Prayer and Reflection**: Spend time in prayer, asking for guidance and clarity. Reflect on the opportunities around you, discerning where God may be calling you to take action. Journaling could be a helpful exercise in articulating your thoughts and prayers.

4. **Connect with Others**: Find a community that shares similar values and beliefs. Connect with those who can

provide encouragement and support as you embark on your journey of action. Consider joining small groups, study sessions, or service organizations.

5. **Embrace Imperfection**: Acknowledge that the journey of faith takes time. There may be successes and failures along the way, but each step matters. Embrace the process and be kind to yourself, knowing that growth often emerges from moments of struggle.

As readers actively engage in these steps, they will begin to understand the transformative power of faith in action. Each story shared, whether of triumph or challenge, reflects the intricate tapestry of life woven together through acts of faith.

Ultimately, taking steps in faith requires trust—trust that even when the path seems unclear, divine guidance is at work. It invites us to lean into our beliefs and engage with the world around us in meaningful ways. Just as Sarah, Marcus, and Leah discovered blessings beyond measure through their acts of faith, so too can each reader foster a transformative legacy of their own. The beauty of faith in action lies not only in the outcomes we achieve but in the relationships we build, the community we nurture, and the light we share with the world.

So, take that step, lean into faith, and trust that your actions, big or small, hold the power to spark change. As you do, remember that you are not walking this journey alone; God walks with you, guiding your steps and illuminating the path ahead. Embrace the call, and step boldly into the life of faith that awaits you.

Community Engagement

Community is more than just a gathering of individuals; it is a tapestry weaved from shared experiences, beliefs, and journeys. When we engage with our communities, we participate in a divine calling, one that transcends the boundaries of our individual lives to create a collective impact that resonates far beyond our immediate circles. For believers, community engagement represents an opportunity to live out their faith in practical ways, serving others and demonstrating God's love in action.

As I reflect on my own experiences, I recall a series of community service projects that profoundly shaped my faith and strengthened my connection to those around me. One such occasion stood out—our church organized a weekly outreach program for the local homeless population. In the beginning, I thought of it merely as an obligation, a task assigned to me. But soon, as I immersed myself in the experience, it became a catalyst for deep spiritual transformation.

Arriving at the community center, I encountered a bustling atmosphere filled with volunteers eager to serve. As we prepared to distribute food and clothing, I found myself engaging in conversations with people from all walks of life. Initially hesitant, I quickly learned that these individuals bore stories of struggle, resilience, and hope. One gentleman in particular, Marcus, struck me with his vibrant personality and infectious laughter, despite the profound hardships he faced. Our conversations revealed his dreams of pursuing his art amid his circumstances, illustrating an unmistakable spark of humanity.

As I served alongside my fellow church members, I began to grasp the essence of community engagement—it is about building relationships, fostering understanding, and loving one another as Christ loves us. This echoed a familiar verse from Galatians 5:13, which reminds us to "serve one another humbly in love." Through service, I realized that I was not just offering help; I was inviting others into a mutual journey of faith.

In Acts 2:44-47, we see the early church living in harmony, sharing everything, and supporting one another. This biblical model of community living serves as an ideal that many faith communities strive for today. When we actively engage in serving others, the act of giving transcends mere charity; it becomes an expression of our faith in action. Our deeds amplify the message of love and hope that we are called to share.

Marcus taught me how healing can begin in the most unexpected ways. After several weeks of conversation, he invited me to an art exhibit he was showcasing at a local gallery. To my surprise, his vibrant depictions of life on the streets captivated an audience that far exceeded my expectations. Seeing him share his art not only deepened my respect for his journey but also reinforced my belief that each member of our community has something valuable to contribute. No one is insignificant; each person's story matters. This realization shifted my perspective on service; it became more about partnership and empathy than about giving.

This experience also prompted me to consider how collective action can amplify individual efforts in a faith context. When groups of believers come together for a common cause, their combined energies cultivate a shared spirit of purpose that extends beyond what they could achieve alone. By harnessing our unique strengths—whether it be financial support, time, or specific skill sets—we create a wave of positivity that reverberates through our neighborhoods.

Consider community gardens, a growing phenomenon in many urban areas. A lack of access to fresh produce often affects low-income neighborhoods, exacerbating health issues. When churches or local ministries rally together to establish community gardens, they not only provide healthy food options but also foster community bonds. Participants share responsibilities, laughter, and stories while tending to the earth, thus cultivating not only plants but a sense of belonging and hope.

As a specific example, I remember visiting a community garden initiative hosted by a collaboration of several local churches. Each Sunday afternoon, volunteers from various backgrounds—young families, elders, and youth groups—came together to cultivate the garden. Working side by side with my neighbors, we learned about agriculture from seasoned gardeners, while sharing recipes and our struggles and celebrations of faith.

Through these interactions, I witnessed individuals stepping outside of their comfort zones, being vulnerable, and forming relationships grounded in love and support. The garden became a vibrant symbol of hope, resilience, and transformation. It dawned on me that faith in action was a living testament to God's promise to care for His creation, and every effort made within the garden reflected that belief.

Engaging in community service not only nurtures relationships with others but also enriches our own faith. The challenges we face in outreach take us on a deeper journey of self-discovery and reliance on God. Sharing faith through communal service can create an environment where the beauty of Christ's love is palpable, transforming both the giver and the receiver.

Engagement in community necessitates that we cultivate a listening heart, one that recognizes the unique needs of those around us. Listening is an act of love; it brings us closer to understanding the challenges our neighbors face. Organizations such as outreach ministries or food banks require more than just volunteers; they seek partnerships with individuals committed to community development and compassionate action.

For those who may be hesitant to step into community engagement, here are some practical suggestions to begin your journey:

1. **Research Local Opportunities**: Spend time exploring local ministries, outreach programs, and nonprofit organizations. Research what resonates with you, and consider how your skills and passions align with their missions. Websites, social media, and community boards are great places to find current needs.

2. **Start Small**: Engaging in community service doesn't need to be a massive commitment. Begin with one-time events or occasional volunteer opportunities. Attend a meal service, participate in a fundraiser, or join a clean-up day at a local park. These small steps can lead to greater involvement.

3. **Leverage Your Gifts**: Every person has unique talents and experiences that can enrich the community. Identify what you can bring to the table—whether it's teaching, mentoring, networking, or simply being a listening ear. Your contribution could be the spark that encourages others to join in.

4. **Build Relationships**: Once you become involved, take the time to build relationships within the community. Engaging in conversations with those you serve and fellow volunteers helps forge connections. Empowering relationships help break down barriers and create an environment where transformation occurs.

5. **Incorporate Prayer**: As we engage in community service, prayer is vital. Invite God into your plans and seek His guidance on how to best serve. Pray for the individuals and families you are helping, as well as for the volunteers around you. A prayerful approach invigorates our actions and strengthens our resolve.

6. **Encourage Others**: Share your experiences and invite

friends and family to join you in community service. Encourage conversations about what moved you and how it empowered your faith journey. Collective engagement spreads spreading enthusiasm and compassion—a ripple effect of love.

7. **Stay Committed**: Consistency is key in community engagement. Make it a point to commit regularly to an organization or initiative. Whether it's monthly or biweekly, consistent participation allows relationships to form and deepens the impact of your efforts.

8. **Reflect on Experiences**: After each engagement, take time to reflect on what you learned and how it influenced your faith. Journaling your thoughts aids in recognizing the growth within you and the transformation within others. Reflective practices can deepen your understanding of God's presence in service.

9. **Seek Feedback and Adapt**: As you navigate your journey, remain open to feedback from fellow volunteers and community members. Adapt your approach as you learn more about the needs and dynamics of the communities you serve. Flexibility arises from a posture of humility, allowing God to redirect your steps.

10. **Celebrate Wins**: Acknowledge the milestones, no matter how small. Whether through shared stories, gatherings, or social media shout-outs, celebrating victories fosters joy and motivates further engagement. Your faith journey thrives amidst encouragement and community recognition.

Ultimately, community engagement is an ongoing journey that transforms all involved; it is a testament to the faith we hold dear. The interconnectedness that develops as a result of standing together in service amplifies our collective impact. As faith becomes action, we embody God's love, illuminating the darkness and offering hope to those around us.

As we step into our communities, let us remember the words from Philippians 2:4: "Let each of you look not only to his own interests but also to the interests of others." In doing so, we fulfill our calling to love and serve in tangible ways. The ripple effect of our engagement can inspire a movement of faith in action, building a legacy of trust, support, and connection for generations to come. Let our faith be the driving force behind our engagement, transforming hearts through the power of community.

Stories of Transformation

The sun dipped low in the sky, casting a warm golden hue over the gathering at the community center. Voices mingled in the air as people from all walks of life came together to share their stories. They were united by an unseen thread—faith in action. Each individual sat with a sparkle in their eye, ready to recount how their lives had been transformed by faith-driven efforts, illustrating the profound impact of putting belief into practice.

At the forefront was Miriam, a single mother who turned her struggles into a powerful testimony. With tears shimmering in her eyes, she began her story. Years ago, faced with overwhelming financial hardship after her husband's unexpected departure, she found herself grappling with despair. She recounted a pivotal day when, overwhelmed and feeling defeated, she knelt on her living room floor, praying for guidance. That prayer ignited a fire in her heart, leading her to seek support from her church community.

"I remember walking into the church office," she shared. "I felt a mix of hope and uncertainty. But when I explained my situation, the pastor didn't just offer words of encouragement; he rallied the congregation. Within a week, we had a meal train set up, and individuals stepped forward to help with my bills."

Miriam's voice grew steadier as she continued, "That experience transformed my faith. I went from being a passive member of the church to an active participant. It became clear to me that faith isn't just a personal journey; it thrives in the community. So, I started volunteering, helping others who faced financial struggles just like I had. This cycle of giving and receiving became a cornerstone of my faith life."

Her newfound commitment not only lit a path for her but also created ripples in the lives of others. "Each time I helped someone, I felt a piece of my own heart heal. This is what faith in action looks like—it's not just about prayers but also about hands and hearts working together."

As Miriam finished her story, the room erupted with applause, a testament to the inspiration her journey provided. Among the listeners was David, a former addict who had encountered faith in a transformative way. The weight of his story lay heavy on him, but with a deep breath, he began.

"Faith came to me in the darkest hour of my life," he started, capturing everyone's attention. "After years of battling addiction, I found myself alone in a dingy motel room, contemplating the end. It was there I had an encounter with God that changed everything. I remember crying out, asking for help. Moments later, I felt a profound sense of peace wash over me."

David described how that moment sparked a desire to pursue recovery and rebuild his life. He connected with a local recovery group informed by faith principles, where members supported each other both physically and spiritually. "I began to put my faith into action. It wasn't just about me getting clean; it was about reaching out and helping others. While I was working on myself, I started volunteering at shelters, sharing my story with those who still felt lost."

Crucially, David's journey highlighted the concept of accountability. "I realized that faith is not a solo act; it's intertwined with the community. My transformation sparked something in others too—they began to believe change was possible." His voice rang with positivity, punctuated by the nods of assurance from those who related to his struggle.

As he concluded, people murmured heartfelt affirmations, reinforcing the idea that through faith, even in moments of immense struggle, transformative power can emerge.

Next to speak was Sarah, a teacher whose life was changed by the faith-driven initiative she spearheaded in her school. "As a teacher," she conveyed, "I noticed a gap in mental health support for our students. I began to pray about how I could help them better. One day, inspiration struck. I decided to start an after-school program focused on emotional well-being, using faith-based principles to guide our discussions."

Sarah detailed her journey in establishing the program, highlighting the challenges she faced. Not everyone supported the idea, as some viewed faith as inappropriate in a school setting. "At first, I felt the pressure to tread lightly, to dilute my approach. But then I remembered that my faith taught me to courageously act. So, instead of minimizing my beliefs, I framed the program in a way that emphasized universal values—kindness, empathy, and resilience."

Her perseverance paid off. The program flourished, providing a safe space for students to share their concerns, discuss their faith, and find comfort in community. Such protections often opened doors for healing and dialogue among students who were struggling.

"I witnessed transformations in my students," Sarah continued passionately. "They began to express themselves, share their faith, and support one another. I saw kids, once bogged down by anxiety and loneliness, become leaders, rallying their peers together. This cycle of faith-inspired action didn't just change them; it transformed our entire school culture."

As she concluded her testimony, laughter erupted in the room, and a realization emerged: faith in action has the remarkable capacity to cultivate courage and resilience in both individuals and communities.

The stories shared so far illuminated the profound impact of faith-driven actions in the lives of individuals. Each narrative echoed a common theme—action rooted in belief creates ripples that touch others, fostering profound connection and change.

Next, an older gentleman named Mr. Thompson stood up to share his wisdom. A retired firefighter, he had spent years not only saving lives but also demonstrating how small acts of kindness could mobilize community spirit. "Years ago, during a particularly harsh winter," he recounted, "a family in our neighborhood lost their home to a fire. They were devastated. But I felt the nudge to act. I organized a fundraiser, and the whole community came together."

Mr. Thompson illustrated how his simple action to support the family led to an outpouring of love and generosity. "More than just funds, people brought food, clothing, and even helped them find temporary housing. Faith in action is often about mobilizing support in tough times. It's about pulling together as a community and showing love where it's needed most."

His voice filled with conviction as he stated, "Never underestimate the power of small actions. Sometimes, the simplest gestures create the most significant shifts. In times of trouble, communities come alive when they act on faith."

Each story echoed in the hearts of those present. The crowd felt the inspiration grow within them, connected by the thread of shared experiences. The narratives of Miriam, David, Sarah, and Mr. Thompson painted a rich tapestry of faith in action, illustrating the profound impact it can have on individuals and communities alike.

As the evening unfolded, the Encourager took the stage. With warmth and enthusiasm, they framed the session into a communal sharing circle. "Now, it's your turn," they said gently, gazing upon the audience. "We all have stories—those moments where faith has driven us toward action. Let's create a space where you can share."

The invitation resonated throughout the room. One by one, attendees began to share their testimonies. A woman shared how volunteering in the local soup kitchen had transformed not just the lives of those she served but her own as well. Another young man spoke about how organizing a community garden had fostered relationships in a divided neighborhood, impacting lives beyond just food.

Each testimony wove seamlessly into the narratives that preceded it, reinforcing the idea that faith in action catalyzes change that can reverberate through individual lives and entire communities.

Amid the testimonies filled with awe and vulnerability, one notable story emerged from a teenager named Jenna. "For me," she said, "faith in action came in the form of my school's protest against bullying. I had been bullied for years, and I prayed for courage."

Jenna explained how she decided to take a stand, organizing an event that encouraged her peers to engage in meaningful dialogue about kindness and empathy. "I remember standing before the assembly, trembling, but I held onto the faith that my voice mattered," she remarked. Fa youth generated energy rippled through the crowd, leading to reshaped conversations about bullying and community support.

The ripple effects of all these stories began to converge,

illuminating a truth that resonated deeply within the gathering. As they continued sharing, they grew aware that these stories didn't just stop with them—they represented a collective hope for a better world.

When the evening drew to a close, the Encourager reflected on the testimonies that had been shared. "What we have heard tonight is a reminder that faith translates into action, leaving transformative imprints on individuals and communities alike. Each story reinforces our responsibility to act—whether through kindness, support, or advocacy. And in our actions, we inspire others to do the same."

The community center buzzed with excitement. People lingered, exchanging thoughts about the stories that had touched their hearts. It was clear that faith in action had not only transformed lives but had also fostered deeper connections and a sense of community among those gathered.

As the evening transitioned into night, attendees left inspired. Many departed with plans to engage more actively in their communities, aware that their actions, however small, could echo profoundly through the lives of others.

Each person carried with them the potential to be a catalyst for change, reaffirming that when faith moves beyond belief and into action, it weaves a powerful narrative—one that brings hope, healing, and connection to a world in need. With each step taken in faith, they too could create ripples of transformation, eternally influencing the lives around them.

The Gift of Patience

The Nature of Patience

Patience is often described as a virtuous quality, one that is highly esteemed in both spiritual and secular contexts. Yet, in a world that thrives on instant gratification, mastering the art of patience can feel like an uphill battle. For many, including our guide, the Woman at the Well, patience is not just about waiting; it's about the journey of personal growth, trust, and ultimately, faith. As we explore the nature of patience, we will delve into how it serves as a crucial component of our faith journey, demonstrating that sometimes, the most profound lessons are found in the waiting.

Scripture provides a rich tapestry of illustrations surrounding patience and waiting, shining a light on how God's timing often diverges from human understanding. One of the most well-known verses on the subject is found in Isaiah 40:31, where we are reminded, "But those who hope in the Lord will renew their strength. They will soar on wings like eagles; they will run and not grow weary; they will walk and not be faint." The promise contained in these words encapsulates a truth that resonates deeply: when we place our hope in God, we are granted strength even during periods of waiting.

The comparison of waiting on God to soaring like eagles transforms the act of waiting from a passive experience into an intentional one—an opportunity for renewal and strength. Patience, therefore, becomes not merely the absence of action but a deliberate engagement with God's promises during times of uncertainty or delay. It invites the faithful to shift their focus from the immediate outcome to a deeper reliance on God's timing and higher plans.

As we reflect on the Woman at the Well, we are invited to witness her journey of learning trust amid the complexities of life.

Initially, she encounters Jesus out of a societal obligation—the shame of her past hovering over her like a cloud. However, as her conversation with Jesus unfolds, she begins to realize that her past does not define her. Instead, it reveals the incongruities between what she believed was possible and what God had in store for her.

Through the eyes of the Woman at the Well, we see a powerful lesson in patience emerge. For her, waiting wasn't just a matter of endurance; it became a formative experience that unlocked deeper layers of her faith. Reflecting on her past, she might have considered moments where impatience overshadowed her ability to perceive God's presence. Each relationship that fell short, each rejection she faced, may have instilled within her a desire for immediate resolution. We are often like her, desiring quick answers and immediate change in our lives.

However, God's ways often include periods of waiting that are essential for our growth. The experience of the Woman at the Well exemplifies how faith can flourish in the fertile ground of patience. As she speaks with Jesus, she is endowed with a sense of purpose, igniting a passion to share her testimony with her community. Her patience transformed her initial despair into a catalyst for hope and connection.

In our lives, it is beneficial to reflect on where impatience might hinder our spiritual journeys. Perhaps we find ourselves praying fervently for a resolution to a current struggle—be it a job search, a fractured relationship, or a health crisis—and growing weary of waiting for a sign. It is essential to recognize these moments of impatience, as they are often indicators of where our faith may need to deepen.

The gift of patience is a heart posture that requires cultivation and intentional practice. As we navigate our day-to-day lives, we can adopt small practices to nurture patience. First, we can engage in daily reflections, taking time to journal about our feelings of impatience, identifying triggers that lead us to want immediate answers. By bringing awareness to these emotions, we create space to invite God into our waiting.

Second, we can immerse ourselves in biblical truths about God's timing. Reflecting on scripture can provide encouragement and strength during times of uncertainty. Consider Philippians 4:6-7, which instructs believers not to be anxious about anything but to present their requests to God in prayer, allowing His peace to guard our hearts when we trust in Him. Infused with these reminders, we adopt a mindset that embraces patience as a vital part of our relationship with the divine.

Moreover, meditation and prayer can serve as pathways to cultivate patience. Just as the Woman at the Well learned to trust in God's redemptive plan despite her circumstances, inviting God into our moment of waiting through prayer allows us to find peace as we surrender our worries to Him. As we seek God's guidance, we find comfort in knowing that He is present in our struggles, orchestrating outcomes for our good and His glory.

Being patient does not mean being passive. It signifies active engagement in faith and hope. It is a choice to lean in during moments of waiting rather than pulling away. When impatience grips our hearts, we can pray for the ability to trust in the waiting.

Like the Woman at the Well, we can learn to perceive each waiting moment as an opportunity for God to work in us and through us.

Let us consider other biblical examples where patience played a critical role in shaping faith. The story of Abraham comes to mind, where he waited decades for the fulfillment of God's promise to become a father of nations. Despite the frustrations and setbacks, Abraham's faith grew stronger with each passing year. Hebrews

6:15 highlights this journey, stating, "And so, after waiting patiently, Abraham received what was promised." His patience was not merely about the duration but the deepening relationship he cultivated with God, which fortified his trust.

Perhaps you have experienced a similar stretch of waiting—one that tested your faith. Reflecting on Abraham's journey can invite us to see our challenges through a lens of hope. Each moment spent waiting can draw us closer to understanding God's character and His desires for us.

In focusing on the importance of patience, we must also acknowledge the role of community in fostering this fertile ground. Just as the Woman at the Well found her voice and purpose in her encounter with Jesus, we too can find strength and encouragement in sharing our struggles with trusted friends or support groups within our faith communities. In these spaces, we can offer and receive reminders of God's faithfulness, which nurtures our patience as we collectively wait for the unfolding of His plans.

The journey of faith is multi-dimensional, and cultivating patience is an integral aspect of this beautiful complexity. As we wait, we are invited to lean into God's promises and seek moments of communion with Him. They can sustain us through times of uncertainty and trials. Patience is not merely a stop along the journey; it is an essential part of our faith development, refining our hearts in the process.

Scripture admonitions call us to practice patience in various relationships as well. Colossians 3:12-13 encourages us to bear with one another and forgive one another, emphasizing the need for patience in our interactions. A patient heart reflects God's love and grace, fostering cooperation and peace. As we cultivate patience within our faith communities and personal relationships, we shape an environment of trust, understanding, and acceptance.

Lastly, we must celebrate the growth that emerges from the waiting. Each instance of patience exercised can reveal new insights and blessings. The Woman at the Well undoubtedly experienced transformation through her waiting, emerging as a powerful witness to those around her. Her story ignites hope and empowers us to reflect on the areas of growth we have gained through the seasons of waiting.

Patience, as a gift from God, invites us to embrace our journey—bumpy roads and all. It reminds us that waiting is not an end but a means through which we discover deeper truths about ourselves and our faith. As we contemplate the nature of patience, we can take steps to cultivate it in our hearts and lives, trusting that in our waiting, God is preparing us for something beautiful on the horizon.

As you reflect on your personal journey and the moments where impatience has led you astray, consider how the practice of patience can reshape your faith. Embrace the waiting as sacred ground, a part of the divine experience that molds and transforms. Allow the stories from scripture and the lessons from the Woman at the Well to inspire you, guiding you toward cultivating a patient heart as you journey through life's uncertainties, trusting in God's perfect timing.atience and transformation that accompany it can serve as pillars of strength as we navigate our unique faith journeys. The Woman at the Well's story reminds us that God meets us in our struggles, offering grace and the promise of transformation, even amidst waiting.

In this dynamic interplay of faith and patience, we learn to trust not only in God's timing but also in His design for our lives—showing us that waiting can lead to beautiful new beginnings. The lessons learned in the process are invaluable, shaping our character and nurturing our confidence as we wait expectantly for His promises to unfold. Ultimately, patience becomes an enduring testament to our faith, a beacon of hope illuminating our paths as we navigate the complexities of life.

Lessons from Waiting

The sound of silence often echoed in the Skeptic's heart during moments of waiting. It was a dull thrum—a constant reminder of an unanswered prayer, a pending decision, or a hope that felt impossibly distant. In these times, the Skeptic wrestled with impatience, a feeling akin to gnawing hunger for something more substantial than the thin air of inaction. Little did he know that the lessons learned in these barren valleys of waiting would shape the contours of his faith more than any moment of immediate gratification could.

For the Skeptic, waiting always felt like a test, a trial by fire. Each day felt like a drop in an ocean of uncertainty, where the waves of doubt threatened to drown his resolve. Yet, it was in this throbbing tension between doubt and faith that he discovered dimensions of his spirit he never knew existed. The waiting period, he would later reflect, became a crucible in which his faith could be tempered and refined.

In his youth, the Skeptic often prayed earnestly for clarity. He had grown accustomed to believing that active, fervent prayer would naturally lead to swift answers. However, as his life journey continued, the Skeptic was frequently met with silence. The more he implored, the quieter the heavens seemed. It was during one particularly challenging period of waiting—when his professional life seemed stagnant, and his personal relationships felt fraught— that he came face-to-face with the reality of his impatience.

Trading his quick-tempered demands for a posture of patience was not seamless. The Skeptic often found himself caught in the throes of discontent, wondering why he was being forced down this long road with no apparent destination. Yet, in those moments of frustration, he began to notice subtle changes—the expansive breath of peace that descended when he paused, the soft emergence of thoughts he had previously dismissed as foolish or unfounded. Patience, he would eventually learn, wasn't merely the absence of action but a fruitful waiting, a rich soil from which faith could grow.

The first lesson that unfolded during his waiting periods was the importance of perspective. As days turned into weeks, and weeks into months, the Skeptic became more aware of the narrative playing out around him. Life was not static; rather, it flowed in cycles of seasons and rhythms. Instead of viewing waiting as a void, he began to see it as an avenue for potential growth. Each day spent waiting allowed him the opportunity to cultivate an inner landscape of reflection and awareness.

For example, he started to document his thoughts during moments of waiting. What had begun as a journal filled with lament evolved into a vibrant tapestry of insights about hope, surrender, and the beauty of trusting in an unseen purpose. The Skeptic wrote earnest letters to God describing his doubts, fears, and the small victories he experienced along the way. Through this practice, he recognized that waiting invited introspection, provoking deeper questions about his priorities and faith. He learned to ask himself: What if waiting isn't merely a hindrance but rather a divine invitation to explore uncharted territories of trust?

One pivotal moment occurred while he waited for a response to a crucial job application. The position he sought wasn't just a career step; it represented a longing for validation and purpose. Each day of waiting injected him with doubt—a persistent whisper that questioned his worthiness. Yet, instead of succumbing to despair, he began actively pondering what God might be teaching him in this interlude.

During his self-reflection, the Skeptic unearthed memories of previous moments in his life when he felt particularly delayed—the time he waited for his first love to reciprocate his feelings, or the year dedicated to a graduate program that yielded no immediate returns. In each case, he discovered how the lack of immediate fulfillment had ultimately propelled him into phases of growth, resilience, and perspective-shifting experiences. The pattern began to emerge: waiting was never wasted time but rather a crucial companion in the journey of faith.

Another significant lesson he learned about waiting was that it had the potential to establish deeper connections with others. The Skeptic began to view his waiting as an opportunity to reach out rather than withdraw. Instead of isolating himself in a cocoon of overthought, he spoke candidly with friends about his struggles. Sharing his feelings of impatience created bonds that were surprisingly intimate. Rather than mere casual conversations, these encounters transformed into heartfelt discussions about their individual journeys through uncertainty.

Through these exchanges, the Skeptic illuminated the spaces where vulnerability coexisted with faith. His friends shared their own stories of waiting, offering mutual encouragement and understanding. For the first time, he realized that waiting was not an isolated experience but one that connected him to the broader human experience—a landscape populated by many who grappled with the same tensions between hope and reality, patience and despair.

As the thread of community began to weave into his narrative, the Skeptic also recognized how waiting can allow for deeper communion with God. In his solitary moments of longing, he began to opt for prayer amid silence instead of grasping for answers. He learned that waiting, in itself, could become a practice of faith—a way to cultivate the soil of his spirit. The act of sitting with God in uncertainty cultivated a type of relationship that built trust and familiarity, allowing him to find solace in the stillness.

One memorable morning, while experiencing a particularly poignant episode of waiting, the Skeptic took a walk through the woods near his home. With each step, he found himself reflecting on the seasons of nature. Trees swayed with the wind gracefully, their branches reaching out, yet they bore no foliage during the winter months, appearing barren and lifeless. With time, however, they would blossom with renewed life. This deceptively simple observation connected the Skeptic to the core lesson embedded in every waiting period: the promise of regeneration.

In nature, he observed, waiting was never futile. Instead, it was embedded in a palpable cycle—there was always preparation hidden in the waiting, developing roots underground until they broke through the surface. Patience became an act of anticipation that developed faith in the unseen.

As the Skeptic continued to embrace these moments of waiting and uncertainty, he realized the necessity of building practical strategies to help him navigate through times of stillness with grace. He began to devise routines that encouraged patience, ways to actively involve himself in waiting rather than feeling passive and helpless.

He set small, intentional goals during waiting periods, focusing on cultivating skills or interests he may have sidelined. He learned to immerse himself in creative outlets, exploring art, journaling, and even meditative practices to provide enriching experiences during his waiting time. These activities not only kept his mind engaged but allowed him to discover new facets of his personality, often unveiling aspects he had overlooked in the rush to achieve.

The Skeptic also began to implement gratitude exercises, purposely reflecting on what he could be thankful for in moments of waiting. By focusing on the good, he cultivated a brighter outlook in the midst of uncertainty. Gratitude shifted his perspective from a place of lack to one of abundance, reminding him that even in stillness, blessings and lessons were abundant.

Along the way, he recognized that practicing patience required communal effort. As he engaged more deeply in conversations with his community, he discovered accountability partners—friends who would check in on him during waiting periods, offering encouragement, empathy, and companionship on his journey. He learned that this supportive network kept a sense of hope alive, affirming that he was not alone in the sometimes-overwhelming space of waiting.

In his reflections, the Skeptic became increasingly aware that embracing a mindset of patience opened him up to transformation—beyond the mere act of waiting, it allowed him to reevaluate his relationship with God, others, and himself. He learned that waiting could be the fertile ground for faith to flourish, leading to profound insights that diaphanously illuminated the path ahead.

As he approached a pivotal year marked by significant changes, the Skeptic faced a daunting choice regarding his career trajectory. Instead of allowing anxiety to plague his thoughts, he drew on his lessons from waiting. He settled into a space of reflection, pouring his concerns into prayer and writing. In those still hours, memories of past waiting periods offered both reassurance and comfort.

On the verge of this significant transition, he reignited a commitment to hold faith as a guiding principle. No longer viewing waiting as punishment but as a crucial phase meant to prepare him for deeper spiritual growth, the Skeptic was ready to embrace what lay ahead, come what may.

In the end, the Skeptic discovered an essential truth: patience was not merely a virtue but a doorway into transformation. Each waiting period became an opportunity to cultivate the soil of his heart and soul. While doubt and impatience still crept in at times, he learned to meet them with a sense of curiosity, embracing the lessons they carried.

As he reflected on the interplay between faith and waiting, he understood that it would not always feel easy. Yet, he felt a quiet assurance within—a faith solidified through the very act of waiting that carried him forward.

In closing, he invited readers to embrace their own periods of waiting with grace, knowing that the lessons learned during such times could yield fruit that carried into the seasons of life beyond. The practice of patience could be woven into the fabric of their lives, guiding them toward transformations that only come in the hush of waiting, fostering a deeper faith that would illuminate the way, even when the path remained unclear.

Celebrating God's Timing

As the sun set over a quiet town, John sat on his porch, sipping a cup of tea and reflecting on the several tumultuous years of his life. A renowned architect, he had spent the better part of a decade working tirelessly to build a name for himself. However, the recent economic downturn had left him jobless, grappling with feelings of inadequacy and fear. The initial shock of losing his career had been overwhelming, leaving him questioning his worth and purpose. Yet, in this quiet moment, he felt the stirring of hope that stemmed from the waiting.

Waiting is not often celebrated; it is usually viewed as a period of inactivity or stagnation. However, what John discovered during his time of waiting was that it could also be a season for growth, healing, and eventual blessings. For months, he navigated the labyrinth of self-doubt, applying for jobs, reaching out to connections, and sending out portfolios. Each rejection felt like a blow to his dreams, but as time passed, he learned to lean into the stillness, seeking solace in his faith.

Moreover, his waiting led him to reconnect with his family, spending evenings around the dinner table, exchanging stories, laughter, and memories that often went overlooked in the race of life. When one night, an old family friend mentioned their desire to build a community center, John was suddenly filled with an inspiration that had eluded him for far too long. This project rekindled his passion for design, and the community spirit reminded him that his worth was not solely measured by professional success.

Around the same time, Sarah, a single mother of two, was experiencing her own waiting period. After a bitter divorce, she found herself stuck in a cycle of fear and uncertainty. The thought of securing a stable future for her children weighed heavily on her shoulders. Every month, as bills piled up and her spirit waned, she would pray fervently, asking God for clarity and direction. Her job as a waitress barely paid the rent, let alone covered necessities, and her dreams of becoming a nurse felt unattainable.

In the depths of her waiting, however, Sarah found strength she never knew she possessed. She began volunteering at a local shelter, providing meals to the less fortunate. The work was exhausting, but it ignited a sense of purpose in her life. Through her service, she developed connections with others facing hardships, and for the first time, she didn't feel entirely alone in her struggle. The experience also solidified her desire to help others, reaffirming her dreams of becoming a nurse.

One evening, amid her bustling waits at the shelter, Sarah encountered a woman who was once in her shoes. This woman took the time to share her journey, offering guidance and resources that lit a spark in Sarah's heart. Eventually, Sarah enrolled in an evening nursing program, allowing her to balance work and family while pursuing her long-standing dream. It wasn't until she finally graduated that Sarah was able to see God's perfect timing in her trials. Looking back, she understood that those years of waiting were a necessary backdrop for the beautiful masterpiece her life was transforming into.

Similarly, Tim's journey of waiting bore fruit in unexpected ways. A high school teacher for over a decade, Tim loved shaping young minds, but after facing unrelenting budget cuts in education, he felt the sting of his profession's limitations. As his contract came to an end, he found himself anxiously browsing job boards while nervously wondering if he would ever find a place where he could genuinely enact change.

During this time, however, Tim took a step back to evaluate what truly mattered in his life. He began to spend time outdoors, hiking through the forests and mountains, filling his mind with nature's beauty. One day, while wandering his favorite trail, Tim stumbled across a group of teenagers gathered around a campfire. They were struggling with their own challenges – family issues, pressure to conform, and feelings of disconnection. Tim felt a tug on his heart to approach them.

Over the course of that summer, Tim organized informal meet-ups with the teens, each offering a space for open dialogue and connection, allowing them to express their feelings. As he shared his experiences of waiting, discovery, and resilience with them, seeds of inspiration were planted in the hearts of those young people. It became clear to him that this was part of his calling, connecting with youth who felt unheard and unimportant.

As the fall approached, Tim was unexpectedly offered a position at a non-profit that focused on youth mentorship, allowing him to turn his passion into a fulfilling career. Reflecting on his past year, he realized his time of waiting was not wasted; it had forged new connections and shaped his understanding of what it meant to be a teacher outside the classroom.

Each of these stories illustrates a vital truth: God's timing is impeccable, even in moments when we struggle to understand. The waiting may not feel productive at the time, but in retrospect, the blessings that emerge often reflect divine orchestration.

God invites us to be patient, reminding us that waiting is not a passive exercise but one that requires faith and trust. When we surrender our plans and expectations to Him, we open ourselves to the possibility of unexpected blessings. Through our stories of waiting, we learn that patience cultivates resilience, hope, and character.

As you reflect on your own journey, take time to celebrate moments of divine timing in your life. Consider those instances where you felt unsure about the future, only to find that, in due time, everything fell into place. Perhaps you, like John, found clarity in unexpected projects or relationships. Or, like Sarah, learned to embrace vulnerability and service during a challenging time. You may even resonate with Tim, discovering purpose through meaningful interactions with others.

To help you capture these reflections, consider journaling your experiences with patience. Here are some questions to guide your thoughts:

1. Can you recall a time when you felt God's presence during a period of waiting? What were the circumstances, and how did it feel to wait on Him?

2. What blessings emerged from your waiting periods that you initially overlooked? How did they shape your journey?

3. Are there areas in your life right now where you feel called to wait? How can you embrace this season with patience and

faith?

4. Reflect on the lessons learned from your waiting. How can they inform your responses to future challenges in your life?

By engaging with these questions, you not only acknowledge the beauty of God's timing in your past but also invite peace and acceptance into your current seasons of waiting.

As we collectively celebrate God's perfect timing in our lives, we recognize that waiting is just as much a part of faith as action. Embracing patience allows us to grow and thrive, preparing our hearts to receive the blessings created in the crucible of time. And so, while waiting may challenge our horizon of understanding, it is within that horizon we often discover the boundless possibilities of God's love, grace, and timing.

Finding Peace in Prayer

The Power of Prayer

The sun had barely risen, casting a gentle glow over the landscape, when Sarah found herself seated at her kitchen table, eyes closed, hands folded as she leaned into the silence of the early morning. For years, prayer had been a refuge for her, a practice that transformed her tumultuous thoughts into a cohesive dialogue with the divine. Today was no different. As she breathed in the aroma of freshly brewed coffee, she felt an overwhelming sense of gratitude wash over her, carried by the simple act of reaching out to God in prayer.

From a young age, Sarah had been taught that prayer was more than just reciting words or following a routine; it was a powerful connection to the heart of God. A lifeline that grounded her during storms and illuminated her path in darkness. Yet, it was also a journey—a gradual unfolding of trust that grew deeper with each conversation held in the quiet moments of her life.

Throughout the scriptures, we are encouraged time and again to pray. Paul writes in Philippians 4:6-7, "Do not be anxious about anything, but in every situation, by prayer and petition, with thanksgiving, present your requests to God. And the peace of God, which transcends all understanding, will guard your hearts and your minds in Christ Jesus." This scripture encapsulates the essence of prayer: it is an invitation to release our anxieties and embrace the peace that can only come from trusting in God.

In a world filled with uncertainty, the transformative power of prayer is a profound assurance that reverberates in the hearts of believers. Consider the testimony of David, who faced monumental challenges as a young shepherd. With enemies encroaching upon him, he often turned to prayer, seeking guidance and strength. In his

Psalms, we find echoes of his struggles and victories, a testament to how prayer became the framework for his faith. As he prayed, the Lord poured out His comfort and fortitude, shaping David into a leader who could shepherd God's people with wisdom.

David once remarked, "I sought the Lord, and he answered me; he delivered me from all my fears" (Psalm 34:4). This deliverance was not just from external threats but from the swirling doubts and fears that can consume one's spirit. David's experience illustrates how prayer can anchor us, helping us navigate life's tumult with a solid foundation of trust.

Then there is Maria's story, a heartfelt reminder of the power of prayer in overcoming personal trials. A single mother raising two children with limited resources, Maria found herself at a crossroads when she lost her job. In despair, she turned to prayer, pouring out her fears and uncertainties before God. Each day, she committed to spending time in prayer, seeking His guidance and a renewed sense of hope.

As the weeks wore on, Maria began to notice a change within herself. Although her circumstances remained daunting, her perspective shifted. The clarity she gained from prayer opened her heart to opportunities she had previously overlooked. She began volunteering at a local community center, where she not only found a supportive network but also discovered a new passion for helping others. God eventually opened doors for her in a new job, a position she felt was tailor-made for her skills.

Maria's testimony exemplifies how prayer can lead to transformative action in our lives, revealing pathways toward solutions that might seem invisible in times of difficulty. She often reminds others, "Prayer doesn't just change situations; it profoundly changes us." Her words resonate with truth, highlighting prayer as the conduit through which God invites us into deeper understanding and awareness.

As we explore these personal accounts, we see that prayer transcends our circumstances; it is a lifeline that connects us to God's infinite wisdom and love. The book James, the brother of Jesus, encourages us to cultivate a prayerful life as well: "Is anyone among you in trouble? Let them pray. Is anyone happy? Let them sing songs of praise" (James 5:13). These dual prompts reflect the expansive nature of prayer—it serves as a response to both our adversities and our victories, reminding us that every moment of our lives can be enriched by engaging with God.

Not only does prayer anchor us personally, but it also has the power to bring communities together. Take the story of a small church in a tight-knit community, facing the loss of a beloved pastor. The congregation was devastated, struggling to find a sense of direction amidst their grief. Together, they began to hold prayer meetings, deciding to bring their collective fears, hopes, and questions before God.

Through their commitment to pray as a united body, the members began to experience remarkable shifts. As they poured out their hearts, they found healing not only individually but as a community. Members who felt disconnected found solace in shared burdens and joys, and they began to carry each other's prayers into their daily lives, strengthening their spiritual bonds. This small act of faithful prayer transformed their mourning into a purpose-driven mission, and they emerged from the valley of despair with renewed vigor and direction.

Communal prayer, like the individual practice, emphasizes the significance of trust. By carrying each other's burdens before God, we reflect His love and grace, creating a tapestry of faith that intertwines our lives. Jesus Himself emphasized the power of prayer among believers, declaring, "For where two or three gather in my name, there am I with them" (Matthew 18:20). These words serve as an assurance that prayer binds us together; it creates a sacred space for collective trust in God's providence.

To enhance one's prayer life, it can be beneficial to create dedicated spaces and times for prayer. For Sarah, her morning routine became a sacred hour. It was in that moment of stillness that she felt closest to God, her heart open and receptive to His leading. Establishing a consistent prayer time allows for meaningful engagement, creating a rhythm that fosters deeper trust.

In addition to setting aside time, it can be helpful to write prayers down. Journaling provides a tangible way to document our conversations with God—a practice that invites reflection and encourages us to see how our prayers align with the unfolding story of our lives. Sarah often scribbled her thoughts in a leather-bound journal, meticulously flowing words onto the pages. On days when her faith wavered, she would return to those entries, recollecting the ways God responded to her petitions and praise.

Scripture also serves as a powerful tool in prayer. By integrating biblical passages into our dialogue with God, we align our hearts with His promises. By praying the scriptures, we not only enrich our conversations but also deepen our understanding of His character. For instance, praying Psalm 23 reminds us of God's unfailing presence and guidance. "The Lord is my shepherd; I shall not want," is more than a declaration. It becomes a prayerful assertion we can embody in our trust of God's provision.

To develop a robust prayer practice, one can explore various forms of prayer. Each has the potential to deepen the conversation we share with God. For example, intercessory prayer, which involves praying on behalf of others, fosters empathy and connection. It turns our focus outward, allowing us to be conduits of God's love and grace in the lives of those around us.

Contemplative or silent prayer offers another avenue to deepen our trust in God. In these moments of quietude, we create space for God to speak into our lives, revealing insights that often get lost in the busyness. Jesus modeled this when He withdrew to solitary places to pray, echoing the importance of retreating to hear the quiet whispers of the divine.

Another valuable practice is praying with gratitude. In the chaos of life, we can become fixated on our problems and forget to recognize God's blessings. By starting our prayers with gratitude, we shift our focus, aligning our hearts with the abundance of His grace instead of the scarcity of our worries. Sarah incorporated gratitude into her prayers, choosing to list three things she was thankful for each morning. Over time, she noticed a profound change in her outlook on life; her prayers became laced with joy rather than anxiety.

Furthermore, setting intentions for prayer can guide our focus. One evening, after a long day, Maria found herself overwhelmed with anxiety. Before she began to pray, she took a moment to settle her thoughts, asking God for clarity and peace. With each word she spoke in prayer, she felt the tension diminish, allowing her trust in God to surface.

As we explore the multifaceted nature of prayer, we see it as a deeply personal and communal journey, intricately woven into the fabric of our faith. It is not merely a practice; it is a relationship—a two-way dialogue with the Creator of the universe who invites us to pour out our hearts and anxieties.

In closing, I urge you to embrace the transformative power of prayer in your own life. Let it serve as a beacon, guiding you through trials and triumphs alike. Each time you come to God in prayer, remember that you are fostering a connection that strengthens your trust and deepens your faith. Prayer invites you to witness the hand of God at work not only in your life but in the lives of those around you.

Consider how you can cultivate a more intentional prayer practice. Create time and space, journal your prayers, and incorporate scriptures that resonate with your heart. Engage in communal prayer and witness the unity and strength it brings.

The power of prayer lies in its ability to transcend our understanding, bridging the gap between us and our Creator. It is an invitation not merely to speak but to listen, to trust, and to build faith that flourishes in the quiet spaces between our words. As you embark on this journey, may you find peace in prayer, allow it to lift you in times of struggle, and celebrate the unyielding presence of God that envelops you through each prayerful moment.

Creating a Prayer Routine

In today's fast-paced world, finding the time for prayer can often seem like a daunting challenge. The demands of daily life—work, family obligations, and the constant stream of notifications from our devices—can easily push prayer to the margins of our schedules. Yet, when we prioritize a consistent prayer routine, we open a pathway to deeper connection with God, clarity in our lives, and peace amidst the chaos. This is a journey that is both personal and communal, one where the practices of many can inspire the spiritual growth of individuals.

The Encourager, a cherished character in our community, has discovered over the years that a structured approach to prayer can be transformative. Their faith has been greatly strengthened through the regular practice of different types of prayer, and they are excited to share their experiences—both the struggles and the triumphs—with you.

To begin crafting your own prayer routine, think of it as building a sacred space within the fabric of your daily life. While every person's routine will look different based on their unique circumstances and preferences, the foundation should remain consistent. The first step in establishing a prayer routine is identifying a specific time of day to dedicate to prayer. Consistency is key. Whether it's early in the morning before the world awakens, during a lunch break, or in the quiet of the evening, setting aside a particular time will help create that sacred routine.

The Encourager shares, "I began by committing to just five minutes each morning. It felt small, but over time, those minutes expanded into a half-hour, and my thoughts transformed from fleeting worries to deep conversations with God. The more I prayed, the more I craved that connection." This initial commitment laid the groundwork for a growing habit that not only shaped their day but also deepened their understanding and relationship with God.

You might find it helpful to use a planner or a digital calendar to block out this sacred time. Not only will this help you stay accountable, but it will also serve as a reminder that this time is a priority. It's essential to treat prayer with the same reverence you would a meeting or an event in your professional life.

Next, consider the environment in which you pray. The surroundings can greatly influence your ability to focus and connect. The Encourager mentions finding a particular spot in their home that felt peaceful and inviting. "I turned a corner of my living room into my prayer nook. I added a comfortable chair, a journal, and even a small candle. Sometimes, just sitting in that space would calm my mind before I even began to pray," they reflected.

Creating a physically comforting and pleasant space can enhance your prayer time. Surround yourself with items that inspire you—perhaps a Bible, meaningful images, or icons that resonate with your faith. By designating a space for prayer, you're reinforcing the importance of this practice in your life.

Now that you have identified the time and space, let's explore the various forms of prayer that can shape your routine. You may choose to include thanksgiving, intercession, supplication, and even silence in your approach.

Thanksgiving prayers focus on expressing gratitude for the blessings in your life. Start your prayer time by acknowledging the good things you often take for granted—a home, family, friends, your health, or even the beauty of nature. The Encourager encourages us to begin each prayer session with a heart of gratitude. "I often find that starting my prayers with thanksgiving sets the tone for the rest of my time. It shifts my perspective from what I don't have to what I am already blessed with," they advise.

Intercessory prayer is the act of praying on behalf of others. This is a powerful practice that encourages community and connection. You might keep a list of friends, family, or even strangers who need prayer, allowing you to focus on their needs specifically. "I keep a prayer journal where I jot down the names and circumstances of those I'm praying for. Each week, I revisit that list, praising God for updates and asking for guidance on difficult situations," the Encourager noted.

Supplication, or asking God for your own needs, should also be a part of your prayer life. This can be a space to express your fears, desires, and struggles. It's important to remember that God invites us to lay our requests before Him. The process of articulating our needs can also facilitate deeper reflection and insight into our own lives.

Silence is an often-overlooked aspect of prayer. Taking time to listen can be just as valuable, if not more so, than the words we speak. Encourager reminds us, "There are days when I simply sit in silence, opening my heart to whatever God wishes to impart. It is in those moments that I often receive the greatest peace and understanding."

Inclusion of all these elements—thanksgiving, intercession, supplication, and silence—can make your prayer routine rich and fulfilling, providing a wide spectrum of connection with God.

To help you structure your prayer time, we have included some templates and prompts that might resonate with you as you embark on this journey. Feel free to adapt these to fit your personal style and preferences.

for.

Sample Prayer Schedule:

- **Morning (10-15 minutes)**
- **Thanksgiving:** Write down three things you are thankful
- **Quiet Reflection:** Spend 2-3 minutes in silence, inviting God into your day.
- - **Supplication:** Present your personal needs or concerns to God.
- **Midday (5-10 minutes)**
- **Intercession:** Pray for 1-3 specific individuals or groups in need.
- -**Prayer Journal:** Jot down any break throughs or moments you feel called to expand on later.
- **Evening (10-15 minutes)**
- - **Reflect on the Day:** What were moments of grace?
- Where did you struggle?
- - **Planning:** Acknowledge what's coming the next day that you want to focus on in prayer.

Prayer Prompts:

1. "God, what is the best way to express gratitude for today's experiences?"

2. "Who in my life needs your healing touch today, and how can I support them?"

3. "What fears do I need to surrender to You, Lord?"

4. "Guide me in understanding how to patiently await Your timing."

By utilizing these templates, you can create a personalized prayer schedule that evolves with your faith journey. The key is to remain flexible; some days you might feel led to spend more time in one area than another, and that's perfectly okay.

It's also important to approach prayer without the stress of perfectionism. Your prayers don't need to be eloquent or perfectly structured. God desires your heart's authenticity above all. "There will be days when the words come easily and others where they don't. Just show up. God meets you where you are," advises the Encourager.

As you begin this journey, remember to be patient with yourself. Establishing a new routine takes time, and there will undoubtedly be days where it feels harder to pray than others. Life can be chaotic, and it's easy to let distractions creep in, causing us to skip prayer or rush through it. Acknowledge these moments without guilt; they are part of the faith journey.

Consider setting reminders on your phone or placing sticky notes in places you frequently visit as visual cues to pause and pray. You might even involve friends or family in this practice, holding each other accountable in your prayer journeys and encouraging collective prayer as a means of deepening your connections with one another and with God.

Finally, celebrate the small victories as you cultivate your prayer routine. Every time you prioritize prayer, you're laying brick upon brick in the foundation of your faith. Keeping a gratitude or prayer journal can also help illustrate your growth over time, allowing you to look back on answered prayers and the ways you've seen God at work in your life.

As you engage with your own established routine, let it become a transformative practice—one that encourages you to dive deeper into your relationship with God while providing a wellspring of peace amid the trials of life.

Prayer, when approached consistently and earnestly, can become one of the most enriching aspects of your faith journey. The Encourager says it best: "Prayer is not a task; it's a privilege. Embrace it as such, and watch how your heart expands in trust and understanding." Allow this routine to be a breath of fresh air in your spiritual life, nurturing your soul and inviting God into every moment.

Remember, the journey of establishing a prayer routine is just that—a journey. Take it one step at a time and allow the rhythm of prayer to integrate beautifully into the everyday tapestry of your life. Each moment spent in prayer is an investment in your faith, your peace, and your connection to God. Ultimately, it will lead to the vibrant and rich life you have been searching for.

Prayer as a Means of Reflection

In the quiet moments of the day, when the world outside stills and the hustle fades into a soft hum, there lies an opportunity for reflection. Prayer has often been viewed as a means of petitioning God, a way to present our requests and desires, but it can also be a profound tool for self-discovery. As believers, engaging in prayer extends beyond simply expressing our needs; it offers us a moment to delve deep within ourselves, uncover hidden truths, and gain clarity in our lives. Through intimate conversation with God, our hearts can emerge transformed, allowing us to explore our fears, hopes, and dreams on our faith journeys.

Think of prayer as a mirror that reflects not only our desires but also the state of our hearts and minds. It holds a space for honesty, allowing us to confront emotions that we often suppress or ignore. By bringing our raw, unfiltered selves before God, we engage in a dialogue that fosters genuine reflection. This dialogue can take many forms—silent meditation, spoken words, or even the written expression of thoughts and feelings.

Consider the Woman at the Well, a pivotal figure in scripture whose prayerful encounter with Jesus was not merely a transactional exchange of requests. Rather, it was a profound moment of revelation and self-awareness. As she conversed with Jesus, her past unfolded before her, and in that sacred space, she confronted her fears and doubts. Through her dialogue, she discovered a new identity—one of acceptance and belonging. Her experience illustrates how prayer can lead to deeper insights into our true selves.

Similarly, we can invite readers on this journey of discovery, encouraging them to approach prayer not just as a ritual, but as an act of exploration. Engaging with God in prayer opens the door to the heart, where hidden fears await acknowledgment and hopeful dreams yearn for expression. It is in this intimate connection that we can peel back the layers of our lives and allow God's voice to guide our understanding.

To begin this journey of reflection, readers are invited to engage in reflective prayer exercises designed to illuminate their hearts. One simple yet effective exercise is to take a moment to sit in silence, allowing the surrounding distractions to fade away. In this stillness, let the mind wander, acknowledging thoughts and emotions as they arise without judgment. After a few moments, grab a notebook and pen, and write down what comes to mind. This unfiltered expression can reveal insights about fears that have lingered or hopes that have sparked interest, providing a foundation for deeper exploration.

Another powerful exercise is the "Prayer of Examen," a practice popularized by Ignatian spirituality. It is an introspective prayer that guides individuals to reflect upon their day, recognize God's presence, and examine moments of gratitude, failure, and growth. By retracing the steps of the day, readers discover patterns in their emotions, reactions, and choices. This practice highlights God's relentless pursuit of our hearts and encourages us to invite Him into every aspect of our lives, welcoming Him into the mundane as well as the extraordinary.

During the prayer of examen, participants may find it fruitful to frame their reflections around the themes of gratitude, recognition, and resolution. Begin by expressing thanksgiving for the experiences of the day, however small they may seem. Perhaps it is a kind word exchanged with a stranger or the warmth of the sun on their skin. Acknowledging these blessings cultivates recognition of God's presence throughout the day and helps ground individuals in their faith foundation.

Next, in a spirit of recognition, readers are encouraged to explore moments when they felt distant from God or encountered challenges. Reflecting on these pivotal moments can often reveal underlying fears— fears of failure, rejection, or inadequacy. Instead of glossing over them, readers are invited to name these fears in their prayers, drawing them into the light and releasing the weight they hold. This act of surrender and recognition creates a space where God can speak truth over these fears, guiding individuals toward healing and understanding.

Finally, in the resolution phase, readers can set intentions for the coming days. They may ask themselves how they can bring their experiences and learning into future actions. This exercise not only reinforces the transformative nature of prayer but also provides a roadmap for their spiritual growth, reminding them that prayer is not just about seeking but also about becoming.

As readers embark on their reflective journey, they may find it helpful to keep a prayer journal. This journal can serve as a sacred space—one where aspirations and reflections can unfold. Daily or weekly entries documenting insights, fears, or dreams help to clarify thoughts, providing a record of growth over time. Re-reading these entries can reveal patterns that might otherwise be overlooked, underscoring the evolving nature of one's faith journey.

It's important to create an atmosphere conducive to this kind of reflective prayer. Perhaps designate a specific spot in the home, a quiet corner where distractions can be minimized. Fill this space with items that inspire, such as nature elements, inspirational quotes, or spiritual literature. Creating a beautiful refuge for prayer will foster a sense of sacredness, inviting God into every encounter.

Additionally, prayer should never be a solitary act. It flourishes in community and shared experience. As individuals engage in prayerful reflection, they can connect with others who are on their faith journeys, sharing insights, fears, and victories alike. Group reflective prayer can deepen understanding and foster mutual encouragement, as individuals bear witness to one another's growth in faith and the transformative power of vulnerability.

As readers continue to nurture their reflective prayer practices, they may find themselves gaining clarity on their identities and their relationships with others. Prayer has the ability to soften hardened hearts and open eyes to the beauty of vulnerability. That softening creates space for compassion to flow, empowering individuals to let go of anger and bitterness and ultimately inviting healing into their lives.

As this subchapter closes, readers are invited to engage in a prayer prompt. Take a moment to still the heart and mind and find a comfortable position. Close the eyes and take a deep breath, inhaling the presence of God. Begin by asking the Lord to reveal any fears that have been holding them back. Be open to the whispers of God, allowing insights to surface without judgment.

Next, transition to exploring hopes and dreams. What are the desires God has placed on their hearts? What passions ignite excitement within them? Allow these hopes to be expressed in prayer, inviting God into the process and trusting Him to guide their steps moving forward.

Finally, conclude with a prayer of surrender. In this surrender, release control over what the future holds and place trust in God's plan. Invite Him to guide their paths and strengthen their faith. As the prayer comes to an end, take a moment to acknowledge any feelings that arise, be it peace, anxiety, joy, or uncertainty. All feelings are welcome in this encounter with God.

Through the practice of reflective prayer, readers embark on a journey of self-discovery and deeper connection with God. Embracing prayer as a means of reflection allows individuals to explore the depths of their hearts, shedding light on the hopes, fears, and dreams that shape their faith. The journey is not always easy; it may require confronting uncomfortable truths or facing emotional wounds, but therein lies the transformative power of prayer.

It calls believers into intimacy with God, encouraging them to trust in His guiding hand along the way. Through this act of reflection, readers will not only uncover the interwoven fabric of their faith journey but will also discover a profound sense of peace that accompanies honest communion with God. The beauty lies in knowing that within each prayerful moment, there exists an opportunity for growth, healing, and connection—inviting us to take steps into a deeper understanding of ourselves and our Creator.

Community of Believers

The Importance of Fellowship

In the heart of every faith journey lies a truth that resonates deeply within the soul: we are not meant to walk this path alone. The importance of fellowship cannot be overstated, for it is within the embrace of community that we find the strength to confront our doubts, the courage to step into the unknown, and the encouragement to pursue our faith with fervor. As we explore the significance of community in our spiritual journeys, we will discover that it is through fellowship that we cultivate trust, accountability, and mutual support, nourishing our relationship with God and one another.

Throughout scripture, we see God's design for community. Time and again, individuals are called not just as isolated believers but as members of a greater body. In the New Testament, Paul writes in 1 Corinthians 12:12-14, "For just as the body is one and has many members, and all the members of the body, though many, are one body, so it is with Christ. For in one Spirit we were all baptized into one body—Jews or Greeks, slaves or free—and all were made to drink of one Spirit. For the body does not consist of one member but of many." This powerful metaphor illustrates that our individual faith journeys are interconnected, and our spiritual growth is often amplified through the support of others.

Consider the life of Sarah, a member of a small church community. After moving to a new city, Sarah struggled to find her footing, feeling isolated and disconnected from her previous support system. As she sat alone in the church for several weeks, she wondered if she could rebuild the same sense of belonging she had once known. However, upon attending a small group meeting, she experienced a transformation. Surrounded by fellow believers who welcomed her with open arms, Sarah found solace in their shared faith, realizing that this fellowship was the missing piece in her spiritual journey. They offered her not only friendship but accountability, encouraging her to deepen her relationship with God and to explore her gifts within the church. This sense of belonging became a bedrock upon which Sarah anchored her faith, reminding her that she was not alone in her struggles.

Fellowship fosters encouragement. In moments of doubt, when the path ahead seems unclear, it is often the voices of our brothers and sisters in Christ that lift us up. Think of John, a man whose faith had faltered amidst personal challenges. Battling anxiety and depression, he felt a heavy weight pressing down on him, whispering lies of inadequacy and hopelessness. Yet, through the weekly gatherings of his church community, John discovered the power of encouragement. One evening, as he shared his struggles in a circle of trust, several members reached out with words of affirmation, recalling the moments they had seen John's faith shine brightly. Their testimonies reminded him of God's faithfulness and the light he carried within him—even when he could not see it himself.

Accountability also plays a crucial role within the context of fellowship. When we surround ourselves with supportive individuals who share our values and beliefs, we open ourselves up to receiving honest feedback and gentle guidance. Acknowledging our shortcomings becomes easier when we are in a community that fosters vulnerability and trust. Take the example of Lisa, a single mother striving to maintain her faith while navigating the challenges of parenting alone. As she connected with other single parents, Lisa found a group that not only understood her struggles but also held her accountable. They committed to praying for one another and challenging one another to reflect Christ's love in their daily interactions. This accountability reinforced Lisa's resolve to cultivate patience and grace in her parenting journey and deepened her connection to God.

The importance of community is underscored by the shared experiences that bind us together. In the same way that Jesus surrounded Himself with disciples, we too are called to be a source of support for one another. The encouragement and accountability we receive in fellowship are often reciprocated. As we invest in the lives of others, we simultaneously open ourselves to growth. Fellowship reminds us that our faith isn't purely an individual endeavor; rather, it is woven into the fabric of relationships. When we engage with others, we create a tapestry of shared experiences that enriches our individual faith journeys and highlights our collective pursuit of God.

Reflecting on our own faith communities is essential in recognizing the role they play in our lives. We must ask ourselves: how connected are we to those who share our beliefs? Are we engaging with our community in a meaningful way? These questions challenge us to consider how we can invest in our relationships with one another and actively foster the fellowship that reflects God's love. It may require stepping out of our comfort zones, engaging in shared activities, or simply reaching out to someone who seems isolated. Every effort matters, for it contributes to the overall strength of the community.

In times of crisis or uncertainty, the community can act as a lifeline. Many individuals have shared stories of how their faith communities rallied around them during significant hardships. For instance, during a particularly challenging season, David lost his job and faced the burden of financial insecurity. Rather than hiding his struggles, he sought support from his church. The response was overwhelming—a group came together to provide groceries, offer prayer, and even assist with job applications. This experience not only exemplified the community's strength but also reinforced

David's faith. He witnessed firsthand how the body of Christ works to support and uphold its members in their times of need.

Moreover, the collective experiences of fellowship often lead to deeper insights about our faith. As we engage in discussions, share testimonies, and listen to one another, we discover new perspectives that enrich our understanding of God's character. Mary, who had long struggled with feelings of inadequacy, found revelation in a church study group. While discussing the story of the Prodigal Son, she heard others share their interpretations, particularly how the father's embrace led to brokenness being made whole. This communal exploration deepened Mary's understanding of grace and forgiveness, transforming her perspective on her own life in the process. Through the fellowship of others, she realized she too could experience the Father's loving embrace.

As we delve deeper into the significance of community, we must also recognize that it's not always easy to connect with others. In a world that often promotes individualism, seeking fellowship can be met with resistance or fear. We may question whether we truly belong or worry about judgment from others. However, it is crucial to confront these barriers, knowing that vulnerability is often the first step toward authentic connection. When we share our struggles, we pave the way for others to do the same. In doing so, we dismantle the walls of isolation, creating a safe environment in which faith can flourish.

It is important to cultivate spaces within our communities that foster open dialogue and allow for shared burdens. Consider the approach of the early church in Acts 2:44-47, where believers came together, shared their resources, and supported one another. This model can inspire modern faith communities to create similar environments where trust abounds. Open discussions about struggles, doubts, and even joys can lead to stronger connections and a deeper understanding of God's workings in our lives.

As readers reflect on their own faith communities, they may find inspiration in the concept of communal worship. Gathering together in praise and prayer can have a profound impact on our spiritual lives. The collective energy of worship ignites passion and devotion, creating a sacred space for encountering the divine. Think of the times when you've felt uplifted by singing alongside others or moved by the power of prayer in a group setting. These moments remind us that fellowship is a vital component of our worship experience and can lead us to a more profound connection with God.

Amid the challenges that accompany community, it is essential to remember the boundless grace extended to each member. Just as we are flawed, imperfect individuals seeking God, so too are our fellow believers. Embracing this truth means allowing room for grace and understanding, especially when conflicts or misunderstandings arise. Rather than allowing differences to drive a wedge between us, we must strive for reconciliation and unity in our intentions. When we prioritize love and forgiveness, we create a healthy community that mirrors the characteristics of Christ.

In addition to personal reflection, consider practical steps to deepen connections within your faith community. Engaging in small group activities, volunteering together, or initiating prayer chains can encourage bonds to form naturally. By investing time in these relationships, you cultivate a foundation built on trust and love. It may involve stepping outside of your comfort zone, but it will ultimately yield rich rewards as you experience the beauty of fellowship.

Furthermore, don't overlook the importance of being an active participant in the community's life. Share your skills, contribute to the collective mission, and extend your hands in service. Whether organizing outreach initiatives or simply reaching out to check in on a member, your involvement matters. The beauty of community lies in the reciprocal nature of support; by investing in others, you inevitably invest in yourself.

As you reflect on your own journey, consider how your faith experiences have been shaped by the community around you. What memories of encouragement, accountability, and growth stand out? What lessons have you learned from the fellowship you've cultivated? By allowing yourself the space to dig deeper into these experiences, you honor the role of community in your life.

Ultimately, the journey of faith is enhanced by the presence of fellowship. Just as iron sharpens iron, so too do our relationships with one another refine our understanding of God and nurture trust in His plans. As we immerse ourselves in community, we gain insights, find encouragement, and experience accountability that strengthens our resolve to pursue Him wholeheartedly.

In the mosaic of faith, every piece is crucial—the colorful tiles of connection that form a larger picture of love and grace. Through fellowship, we rediscover the beauty of belonging, recognizing we are not solitary figures walking a solitary path. Instead, we are members of one body, intricately woven together by our shared faith. In embracing this community of believers, we enhance our own journeys while uplifting one another toward a deeper, richer relationship with God. So let us step into the warmth of fellowship, knowing we are both strengthened and sanctified through our connection with those who share the same faith. Together, we illuminate the journey of faith, forging ahead as a unified body in Christ.

Building a Supportive Network

In today's fast-paced world, where the hustle and bustle often drown out meaningful connections, the need for a supportive faith network has never been more crucial. As human beings, we are wired for connection; we thrive on relationships that nurture our spirits and cultivate our faith. This subchapter focuses on practical steps for building a supportive network within a faith community, highlighting not only how to engage with others but also how to be that supportive presence for others. The Encourager—a guide who embodies these principles—will illustrate how shared experiences and collective beliefs can forge lasting connections, encouraging readers to actively seek out both the fellowship they need and the ways they can uplift others in their journey of faith.

To start, let's consider the environment in which we find ourselves. The modern age has ushered in advancements that, while convenient, can also create barriers to genuine relationships. Social media can often provide a false sense of connection, leaving us feeling isolated despite having countless online "friends." We can tap our screens and scroll through curated lives, yet still feel a profound sense of disconnection when we put our devices down. This reality underscores the importance of engaging with a community of believers that offers authenticity and depth.

A supportive faith network begins by being intentional about finding the right community. The Encourager emphasizes the importance of looking beyond the superficial layers of a large congregation. While attending services is important, it's within smaller groups—such as Bible studies, prayer circles, or interest-based gatherings—where deeper connections are often formed. The Encourager suggests that readers take these steps to locate and begin engaging with smaller groups:

1. **Identify Interests and Gifts**: Before diving into a community, reflect on your interests and spiritual gifts. Do you have a passion for service, teaching, or worship? By identifying your strengths and interests, you can seek out activities and groups that align with them, allowing you to connect with like-minded individuals who share similar passions. This alignment fosters an environment where authentic relationships can blossom.

2. **Research Local Opportunities**: Take time to explore the various offerings within your local church or community. Many faith communities host events that cater to different demographics—youth groups, women's circles, men's breakfasts, and more. Attend these events with an open heart, for they are often the entry points into smaller, more committed gatherings. Don't hesitate to ask your church office for recommendations on groups that might fit your interests.

3. **Attend a New Event Each Month**: Commit to attending at least one new event or group activity each month. This could be a service project, a fellowship meal, or a workshop. Embrace the discomfort of stepping outside your comfort zone, as these experiences will lead to new relationships. With each interaction, you're not just seeking a community; you are contributing to it.

4. **Be Open to New Connections**: When you attend gatherings, keep an open mind about forming relationships with individuals who may differ from your initial expectations. Every person has a unique story and a contribution to make. The Encourager often recounts how some of their closest friendships emerged from unexpected encounters—be it in a prayer group or through engaging in outreach activities.

5. **Follow Up and Stay Connected**: After meeting someone new, don't shy away from following up. A simple message expressing gratitude for a shared experience or a question about follow-up activities can pave the way for deeper conversations. Consistently reaching out and engaging will reinforce the bond that began with a casual introduction.

After finding a community that feels supportive and encouraging, the next step is actively engaging with it. This is critical to witnessing the transformative power of fellowship. The Encourager advises individuals to consider these steps for participation:

1. **Volunteer Your Time**: One of the best ways to immerse yourself in a community is to volunteer. Whether it's serving in the children's ministry, helping with church maintenance, or organizing outreach programs, offering your time allows you to meet others while contributing to something greater. The act of serving not only strengthens your faith but also deepens your relationships with fellow volunteers.

2. **Share Your Story**: Every individual in faith has a story worth sharing. Open up about your journey, including your struggles, triumphs, and the ways you've seen God work in your life. Authentic sharing fosters trust and allows others to empathize and connect with you on a personal level. When individuals relate to your experiences, it creates a foundation for deeper conversations.

3. **Attend Regularly**: If possible, become a consistent presence within your faith community. Regular attendance allows you to become familiar with others and creates a sense of belonging. Your willingness to engage consistently sends a message to others: you're invested in your community and committed to nurturing relationships.

4. **Be an Active Listener**: Engagement isn't just about sharing your story; it also involves listening to others. Create space for people to share their experiences and concerns. Be genuinely interested in their lives and offer compassionate support. The Encourager often emphasizes that active listening is one of the greatest gifts we can offer one another,

fostering deeper bonds through understanding.

5. **Participate in Community Outreach**: As you engage with your faith community, look for opportunities to partake in outreach efforts. These experiences not only serve the community at large but also solidify your bonds with fellow believers as you work collectively towards a shared goal. The bonds formed in service can be transformative and create a sense of purpose.

While cultivating a supportive network is crucial, becoming a supportive presence within that network is equally important. It's essential to remember that relationships are reciprocal; the more you invest in others, the more enriched your community becomes. The Encourager shares practical ways that readers can uplift their fellow believers:

1. **Be Present**: One of the simplest yet most profound ways to support others is by being present. Attend events, offer a listening ear, and engage with those who are struggling. Your presence can provide comfort and reassurance, reminding individuals that they're not alone in their journeys.

2. **Offer Encouragement**: Small gestures of encouragement can spur someone's faith forward. Compliment another's contributions, offer words of affirmation, or send messages of support during challenging times. Building a culture of encouragement within your community fosters an uplifting environment where everyone feels valued.

3. **Pray for Others**: Make it a priority to pray for members of your community. Establish prayer partners or engage in regular group prayers. Sharing specific prayer requests not only deepens trust but also highlights the community's

commitment to supporting each other spiritually.

4. **Lead by Example**: Model the behavior you wish to see in your community. Share your struggles and victories openly and foster a culture where vulnerability is both accepted and encouraged. When others witness your authentic faith, they'll feel inspired to do the same.

5. **Organize Fellowship Activities**: Take the initiative to organize fellowship gatherings—whether it's a potluck, game night, or community service day. Such events create opportunities for deeper connections and can invite everyone to participate, emphasizing the communal aspect of faith.

6. **Be Mindful of Diversity**: In any community, members come from different backgrounds and experiences. Embrace this diversity, and seek ways to be inclusive of varying perspectives. Encourage conversations that honor each individual's faith journey, demonstrating that everyone has a valuable contribution to make.

7. **Communicate Openly**: Ensure that you are approachable and open to dialogue within your faith community. Honest communication is the cornerstone of any supportive network. Encourage individuals to come to you with their concerns, and give them the safe space to express their feelings and experiences.

Building a supportive network is not a linear process, but rather a continuous, evolving journey adorned with the beautiful complexities of human relationships. Strive to be patient and understanding as connections develop organically. The Encourager reminds us that it takes time for relationships to blossom, and there will be moments of uncertainty along the way. Embrace the imperfection, for those moments often lead to the most profound growth—both individually and within the community.

As you venture forward, remember the essence of faith as community. Recognizing that you are part of a larger whole can provide comfort during trying times. The journey of faith is best traveled alongside others; they can lend support and guidance when challenges arise, celebrating victories alongside you.

The Encourager concludes this subchapter with a reminder that a strong community of believers is built on mutual care and respect. Each individual contributes to the collective story of faith, woven with threads of personal experiences and shared journeys. As you work to find, engage, and support your faith community, you are not merely cultivating a network; you are building a family bound together by love and a shared purpose.

In summary, the path to creating a supportive faith network involves intentionality, participation, and a commitment to uplift one another. By seeking out opportunities for connection and actively engaging with the community, you foster relationships that strengthen not only your own faith but also the faith of those around you. In this ever-shifting world, having a reliable support system within a community of believers is not just beneficial—it is essential for navigating the complexities of life. As you step forward into this journey of connection, remember that both finding support and being supportive are vital parts of a community grounded in faith, love, and mutual perseverance.

Testimonies of Community Impact

In a small town nestled amidst rolling hills, the local church had become more than a building for Sunday services; it transformed into a sanctuary for a community seeking faith, healing, and growth. It was a place where people gathered not only to worship but to build relationships that would support them in their spiritual journeys. The stories that emerged from this community highlight the powerful impact of fellowship on individual lives.

Sara, a young mother struggling with anxiety, attended the church sporadically, feeling lost in her daily battles. The pressures of motherhood weighed heavily on her, leaving her exhausted and questioning her self-worth. One Sunday, as she sat quietly in the back pew, she overheard a small group of women sharing their experiences with mental health. It wasn't just the church's teachings that brought hope to Sara but the vulnerability displayed by those women. They spoke candidly about their struggles with anxiety and depression and how their faith had guided them through these dark times.

With her heart racing, Sara hesitated but eventually mustered enough courage to approach the group after service. What unfolded was a revelation of healing for Sara, as she found not just empathy but actionable advice that helped her navigate her internal battles. The women invited her to their weekly Bible study, and as Sara began to attend, she discovered a safe space to share her fears and receive encouragement. Over time, she learned to pray openly about her anxiety and found comfort in knowing she wasn't alone.

Reflecting on her journey later in a meeting, Sara shared, "Before I joined this group, I felt like I was drowning. I wore a mask of perfection to hide my struggles, but they saw me for who I really was. Their honesty allowed me to be honest, and together we found strength in faith and community."

The transformation of Sara's faith journey illustrates the essence of belonging that a community of believers fosters. As she cultivated relationships within the group, their collective prayers became a lifeline. Week by week, she felt lighter, empowered not just by her faith in God but by the love and support of her church family.

Across town, Michael was another member whose experience

highlighted the communal impact on faith. As a volunteer at the local homeless shelter, he often shared food and meals with those in need. Despite his good intentions, Michael faced deep-seated doubts about whether his efforts made any real difference. One day, a man named James approached him as he was serving lunch. With tears in his eyes, James said, "You don't know what this meal means to me. It's not just about the food; it's that someone cares enough to serve."

This encounter struck Michael profoundly. He learned that acts of service extend beyond physical provision; they touch people's lives in ways he had never considered. The mutual support within the church encouraged him to push forward, to lean into this vocation of service. His doubts transformed into confidence as he began organizing church community days at the shelter, inviting others to join and share their gifts.

"I've seen firsthand how our faith can move mountains," Michael later articulated during a congregation meeting. "When we act together, it's not just a meal we serve; it's hope. It's the message that we believe in a God who cares, and we manifest that through our acts of love." His enthusiasm sparked a wave of participation, inspiring more church members to engage with the community and build a network of support for the homeless population in their town.

As these stories of transformation unfolded, they resonated within the fabric of the church community. People began to see that their individual journeys were interwoven with the experiences of others. The community became a tapestry of faith stretching across ages, backgrounds, and struggles, each thread strengthened by the testimonies of its members.

Elaine, a retired teacher, found herself isolated after losing her husband. The grief enveloped her, and she drifted away from regular church attendance. While cleaning out some old books, she stumbled upon a journal filled with reflections from her years of teaching. Within those pages, she discovered her deep-rooted passion for nurturing the younger generation. One Sunday, Elaine returned to church with a desire to reconnect, but this time she sought a new purpose: mentoring the local youth group.

At first, she was nervous about how the teens would receive her. But during their first meeting, the shared laughter, stories, and discussions on faith melted her apprehension. As the group became more engaged, Elaine found her place in nurturing young hearts. Through her guidance, she witnessed transformations in the lives of those teens, who began to grapple with their questions and doubts about faith openly.

"I think my life is richer now than it has ever been," Elaine expressed to the youth group one evening. "Your energy in this community helps fill the void I felt. You remind me that we grow together in faith, and you inspire me just as much as I hope to inspire you."

This mutual transformational journey reinforced the church's role as a foundation for support. Elaine's experience serves as a reminder that giving back often enriches our own lives, proving that as community members lift one another, they inadvertently elevate their faith.

A powerful example within this community impact is the story of Jason, a teenager with cerebral palsy. Since childhood, he yearned for acceptance but often felt alienated due to his disability. He attended church with his parents but kept to the sidelines. The youth pastor saw something special in him and encouraged him to step out of his comfort zone by participating in a church play. Skeptical at first, Jason joined the drama group, meeting friends who welcomed him unconditionally.

Through rehearsal and shared laughter, Jason's self-esteem blossomed as he discovered his voice on stage. The culmination of the performances brought not only applause but validation. In sharing his stories through drama, his faith journey deepened, and he learned that vulnerability could lead to connection.

"It wasn't just the play; it was the love I felt from everyone involved," Jason recounted at a church family night. "Being part of something bigger showed me that I'm not just defined by my struggles. I can contribute my uniqueness, too."

Jason's newfound confidence spread through the community, inspiring others to embrace their authentic selves. His story became a testament to the importance of inclusion within a faith community, demonstrating how acceptance fosters faith development and strength.

As the church community flourished, they also became known for their outreach activities. During one at-risk youth workshop, a fabricated wall crumbled down between different congregation members and the local youth in attendance. Through dialogue about struggles, dreams, and aspirations, relationships formed. The pastor emphasized this exchange, stating, "We share our faith by opening our hearts to one another. Each of you brings a unique story, and through this connection, we embody Christ's love."

These words echoed throughout the community. Attendees began creating partnerships aimed at empowering local youth. They pooled resources to offer tutoring sessions and mentorship programs. As they worked together toward common goals, the testimonies of community impact rippled. The youth began showing visible improvements in their confidence and academic performance.

Amid these transformations, the worship team celebrated milestones not only in music but also in the personal testimonies of individuals. One young woman, Leah, took to the stage, sharing how her life positively shifted through her community's love. "There's this magic that happens when hearts unite," she said. "We become the hands and feet of Christ, and together, we are stronger."

Leah became a source of inspiration, having taken her past of addiction and recounting how it was through the grace shown to her by the people of the church that she emerged whole again. She inspired others to seek healing and brought several friends from her recovery group to church, creating an overflow of testimonies of the powerful impact of building each other up.

The community's impact was crystal clear. Connections forged in those vulnerable moments of sharing and loving led to numerous stories of restoration and hope. As the congregation gathered to reflect on these experiences, they began prioritizing fellowship more in their programs. They held potlucks, game nights, and group outings to create spaces for connection.

In one gathering, people were encouraged to share their personal experiences within the church community. Stories of resilience, hope, and change continued to emerge. Attendees left inspired to contribute to this environment of growth and transformation.

Many began forming prayer circles to support one another through struggles. These circles nurtured spiritual connections, fostering an atmosphere of trust that complemented their faith journeys. They learned to lean on each other, offering prayers that were genuinely heartfelt and powerful.

As members of the congregation exchanged stories, they grew closer together. They learned life wasn't simply about personal triumphs; it was about lifting others into their own journeys, uniting to move forward together through challenges. The community emerged transformed, understanding that they were imperfect yet beautiful individuals, bonded together through their faith.

Reflections on their faith journeys brought forth a realization that their shared experiences made their lives richer, not just as individuals but as a collective body of believers. The spirit of encouragement resonated within the walls of the church, charging them with the potent reminder that God moved through their hands and voices, through every act of love.

As the subchapter draws to a close, readers are invited to contemplate their own experiences within their faith communities. Exploring the connections they've formed can deepen their understanding of belonging and support.

- Reflect on a time when your community uplifted you during a challenging moment. What impact did those connections have on your faith?

- Consider ways you can contribute to fostering an environment of trust within your community. How might your personal journey inspire others, just as Sara, Michael, Elaine, Jason, and Leah did?

- Journal about the unique gifts and experiences you bring to your faith circle. How can these be shared to strengthen the bonds and grow together in faith?

By embracing stories of community impact, we not only celebrate our own journeys but ignite the flames of faith in others, creating a ripple effect that transforms lives. Each voice matters, and together, we create a symphony of hope that echoes far and wide.

Gratitude as a Faith Builder

The Role of Gratitude

Gratitude is a powerful force that can transform our perception of the world and deepen our faith in God. It is more than mere acknowledgment of our blessings; it is an active recognition of the divine fingerprints in our lives, a conscious choice to focus on the good, and a spiritual practice that aligns our hearts with God's purpose and provision. As we journey through life, we often find ourselves caught in the whirlwind of demands, disappointments, and distractions, making it easy to overlook the countless ways God has been present and active in our lives. Nevertheless, cultivating an attitude of gratitude can lead us back to a place of peace, trust, and renewed faith.

Throughout Scripture, we find numerous references that call us to be thankful. In Ephesians 5:20, Paul exhorts believers to "always give thanks to God the Father for everything, in the name of our Lord Jesus Christ." This verse underscores the comprehensive nature of gratitude; it is not limited to moments of joy or success but extends to every aspect of our lives, including challenges and trials. This invitation to thankfulness encourages us to see beyond our immediate circumstances, fostering a perspective that acknowledges God's sovereignty and goodness, even in adversity.

In Philippians 4:6-7, we are reminded, "Do not be anxious about anything, but in every situation, by prayer and petition, with thanksgiving, present your request to God. And the peace of God, which transcends all understanding, will guard your hearts and your minds in Christ Jesus." Here, gratitude acts as a bridge between our worries and the divine peace that God offers us. When we approach God with a heart full of thanks, our anxieties begin to dissipate, and we open ourselves up to His comforting presence. This passage beautifully illustrates that gratitude is not merely a response to blessings; it is a choice that shapes our relationship with God and allows us to engage with Him more deeply.

Gratitude enhances our awareness of God's constant involvement in our lives. In Colossians 3:15, we read, "Let the peace of Christ rule in your hearts, since as members of one body you were called to peace. And be thankful." Recognizing and acknowledging God's blessings fosters peace within us and enhances our faith. It encourages us to rest in the assurance that we are cared for and loved, reinforcing our trust in God's timing and provision.

As we reflect on gratitude's transformative power, it may help to share personal anecdotes that illustrate its significance in our spiritual journeys. One such story comes from the Devotional Guide, who experienced a profound shift in perspective through the practice of gratitude. After a turbulent season marked by loss and uncertainty, the individual found solace in journaling daily blessings. Each night, before going to bed, they would take time to list at least five aspects of their day that brought joy or comfort.

In the beginning, this practice felt laborious and forced. The burdens of life weighed heavily on their heart, obscuring any immediate sense of gratitude. It was easy to focus on what was going wrong—an unexpected bill, a disagreement with a friend, or feelings of isolation. However, as they persevered in committing these blessings to paper, a gradual change began to take shape. Over time, it became easier to acknowledge even the simplest joys: the warmth of a morning sunbeam, the laughter of a loved one, or the solace in a favorite book. This intentional act of gratitude opened their eyes to the richness of life.

Through this journey of gratitude, the Devotional Guide came to understand that recognizing blessings—including those that initially felt insignificant—had the power to shift their focus away from problems and towards God's provision. Each acknowledgment of blessing reaffirmed their faith and trust in God's character. They began to perceive the subtle ways God was present, weaving together experiences that provided comfort in difficult times.

Scripture emphasizes this journey toward awareness and thankfulness. In Psalm 136, the psalmist opens with an exuberant call: "Give thanks to the Lord, for He is good; His love endures forever." This refrain reinforces the idea that gratitude stems from recognizing God's eternal goodness and faithfulness. It is an acknowledgment that transcends our circumstances, leading us to a deeper understanding that, regardless of what we face, God's love is unwavering.

As we explore gratitude's transformative power, we may find it beneficial to consider specific aspects of our lives that foster a grateful heart. What blessings have we overlooked amid the noise of life? Have we taken time to praise God for the mercy and grace that continually sustain us? Engaging in reflection can can remind us of the myriad of ways God fulfills His promises: through answered prayers, lessons learned from hardships, and cherished relationships. When we take a moment to ponder these aspects, our minds shift from a scarcity mindset, focused on what we lack, to an abundance mindset, appreciating all God has done.

Gratitude also enhances our sense of connection with others. As we acknowledge the love and kindness we receive, we inevitably find ourselves more willing to extend that same grace towards those around us. The act of thanking someone for their support, encouragement, or service can foster deeper relationships, drawing us closer together in community. In Hebrews 10:24-25, we are encouraged to "consider how we may spur one another on toward love and good deeds, not giving up meeting together." As we come together to share our journeys of gratitude, we create a foundation of trust where we can uplift one another and celebrate the blessings God has bestowed upon us.

The Devotional Guide also reflects on the communal aspect of gratitude through their experiences volunteering at a local shelter. Many guests came from difficult backgrounds, carrying burdens that often left them feeling invisible and alone. However, the atmosphere of gratitude among the volunteers created a ripple effect that illuminated their service. The act of thanking each other for their contributions—no matter how small—created a sense of camaraderie. Sharing stories of hope and resilience reminded both volunteers and guests of their inherent worth in God's eyes. In this shared space of gratitude, individuals began to feel seen and appreciated.

Recognizing blessings also provides an avenue for worship. When we approach God with gratitude, we position ourselves to give Him honor and glory. As we reflect on the goodness of God and His unchanging nature, we align our hearts with the psalmist's refrain: "I will give thanks to the Lord with my whole heart; I will recount all of your wonderful deeds" (Psalm 9:1). In this acknowledgment, we engage in an act of worship that celebrates God's faithfulness and allows gratitude to stretch into areas of our lives we may have previously taken for granted.

Another anecdote from the Devotional Guide illustrates the importance of gratitude in the context of worship. During a particularly challenging season, marked by uncertainties and struggles, they found solace in a local worship service. Surrounded by fellow believers, the atmosphere was rich with joyful expressions of thankfulness. The music flowed, and as the congregation sang lyrics about God's faithfulness, the burdens weighing on their heart began to dissipate. Recognition of God's goodness in unison with others cultivated a deeper understanding of His love and presence.

In moments of communal worship, gratitude becomes

contagious. It unlocks a cycle of praise, lifting our spirits and bolstering our faith. When we experience gratitude collectively, we are reminded of God's blessings in our lives, creating a powerful impact that ripples through our communities.

As we delve deeper into the role of gratitude in our faith journeys, it is crucial to recognize the transformative potential of gratitude in our responses to adversity. In difficult times, gratitude can feel elusive, but it is precisely during such moments that it becomes even more essential. When we cultivate a spirit of thankfulness amidst trials, we fuel resilience and fortitude in our faith. James 1:2-4 encourages us, "Consider it pure joy, my brothers and sisters, whenever you face trials of many kinds, because you know that the testing of your faith produces perseverance."

The practice of gratitude amidst tribulation aligns our focus with God's purposes, allowing us to find strength and hope in the midst of uncertainty. By identifying blessings hidden within challenges, we begin to uncover the glimmers of God's faithfulness.

The Devotional Guide recalls a particularly difficult period marked by job loss and financial strain. Initially, anxiety consumed their thoughts, clouding every aspect of their life. Yet, as they gradually leaned into gratitude, they began to recognize the moments of support and kindness from friends and family—time spent in laughter, words of encouragement, and the generosity of a community that rallied around them. By reframing their experience through gratitude, they found renewed hope that transcended their immediate circumstances.

In doing so, they learned that gratitude was not about denying the existence of pain but rather acknowledging God's presence through it. This understanding transformed their faith, fortifying their trust in God's plans—a foundation upon which they built resilience in the midst of trials.

We can also draw insight from the wisdom found in Scripture, where gratitude is interwoven with the notion of trust. In 1 Thessalonians 5:16-18, Paul writes, "Rejoice always, pray continually, give thanks in all circumstances; for this is God's will for you in Christ Jesus." This passage challenges us to embrace gratitude in every aspect of our lives—not just in moments of ease but even in moments of hardship.

Gratitude enhances our trust in God's provision—convincing us that there is always something to be thankful for. By choosing to focus on our blessings, regardless of our circumstances, we embrace a narrative shaped by hope, resilience, and unwavering trust in God's goodness.

As we incorporate gratitude into our daily rhythms, we invite opportunities for reflection and growth. Take time to create a gratitude journal, where you can recount specific blessings you encounter. Consider moments where God's presence felt particularly vivid or where you sensed His comfort during difficult times. Over time, you'll build a collection of experiences that showcase God's unwavering faithfulness—a testament to the transformative power of gratitude.

Invite others into this practice; share your stories of gratitude with friends and family. Create spaces where collective thanksgiving becomes an integral part of your community worship. Let each moment of recognition and appreciation cultivate deeper relationships that foster trust and support.

Gratitude, when embraced, creates an abundant landscape in our hearts, leading to a flourishing faith that grows despite setbacks. We discover that gratitude is not a remedy for hardship but a lens through which we view our experiences, shaping our trust in God and drawing us closer to Him.

As we reflect on our journeys and recognize gratitude's role in nurturing faith, we invite the Holy Spirit to create a deeper hunger within us—to not only acknowledge the blessings around us but to continually seek God in the midst of our trials.

As we close this exploration of gratitude, consider a reflective prayer. Take a moment to quiet your heart, and invite God to illuminate the specific blessings within your life. Ask Him to open your eyes to see the beauty and abundance all around you, even when times feel challenging.

In embracing gratitude, no matter the circumstance, we are continually drawn closer to the heart of God, where our faith blossoms and deepens—an invitation to trust in the unshakeable goodness of His presence. Gratitude nurtures our attitudes, reshaping our hearts, and prompting us to embrace the journey of faith with renewed zeal. As we cultivate a grateful spirit, we emerge transformed, revealing the profound connection between faith and gratitude—a tapestry woven by grace that empowers us to trust, love, and serve.

Practicing Daily Gratitude

Gratitude is a practice, an intentional choice to recognize and appreciate the myriad of blessings in our lives, and when approached with consistency, it can evolve into a powerful faith-building tool. In this subchapter, we will explore practical exercises for cultivating gratitude, share inspiring testimonials from characters who have experienced profound spiritual growth through this practice, and provide actionable tips to seamlessly incorporate gratitude into your daily routine. Each step and reflection brings us closer to understanding how gratitude can strengthen our faith and enhance our relationship with God.

At the heart of this exploration is the concept of a gratitude journal—a dedicated space to record our blessings, reflections, and prayers. Keeping a gratitude journal transforms fleeting moments of thankfulness into tangible records of appreciation. It allows us to shift our focus from what we lack to what we already possess, nurturing a more profound sense of contentment and awareness. To get started, here are some daily prompts that can guide your reflections:

1. **What am I grateful for today?** Write down three things that brought you joy or comfort, no matter how small. It could be a warm cup of coffee, a kind word from a friend, or the beauty of a sunrise.

2. **Reflect on a challenge:** Consider a recent difficulty. What did you learn from it? How did it ultimately lead to growth or a deeper understanding of God's presence in your life?

3. **Gratitude for relationships:** Think about the people in your life. Who made a positive impact today? Write a note of thanks—whether in your journal or a message to them— expressing your appreciation.

4. **Nature's gifts:** Spend a moment in nature and observe your surroundings. What aspects of nature do you appreciate? Reflect on how God's creation surrounds and nurtures us daily.

5. **Milestones of faith:** Write about a moment in your faith journey that made you feel especially close to God. What were the circumstances, and how did they impact your trust in Him?

By using these prompts, your gratitude journal will become a powerful spiritual tool. Consistency is key—set aside a few minutes each day to facilitate this practice. As you begin to note your blessings and reflections, you'll soon notice subtle shifts in your outlook, enriching your faith and daily experience.

Woman at the well walking by FAITH

In sharing how gratitude can lead to spiritual growth, we turn to the testimonials of our characters—the Woman at the Well and the Encourager—whose journeys reveal the profound impact of cultivating gratitude in their lives.

The Woman at the Well, whose transformative encounter with Jesus unraveled societal norms and personal barriers, found gratitude in the most unexpected places. After feeling the weight of her past, her new faith illuminated her journey, showcasing the power of gratitude in overcoming doubt and despair. Upon starting her gratitude journal, she wrote about her experience of acceptance and love from Christ. She recalled the moment Jesus engaged her in conversation, stripping away her shame and filling her heart with grace. Each entry became a manifesto of her faith, affirming her identity and purpose in God's family.

"Gratitude transformed how I viewed my past," she reflects. "Instead of focusing on shame, I began to count my blessings—my community, my purpose, that conversation at the well. In those moments of reflection, I realized that God had always been there, even in the darkness."

Similarly, the Encourager's journey emphasizes how gratitude shifted his perspective amid life's trials. He often faced challenging circumstances that tested his faith. One day, feeling overwhelmed by personal struggles, he decided to commit to daily gratitude practices. Inspired by the stories of those around him, he noted each blessing from day to day.

"Incorporating gratitude into my routine allowed me to see beyond the trials," he shares. "Every small victory became a testament to God's faithfulness. My perspective shifted, and I began to recognize that even in chaos, there is beauty to be found—like the laughter of my children, the warmth of the sun, and the love of my wife. These daily reminders kept my faith alive, even in turbulent seasons."

As we move forward, let us explore practical steps to establish gratitude as a vital part of our daily lives.

1. **Consistency is Key:** Aim for a specific time each day to write in your gratitude journal. Whether it's the morning or night, find a slot that works best for you. Setting a reminder can help to build a lasting habit.

2. **Create a Gratitude Jar:** Each day, write down one thing you are grateful for on a slip of paper and place it in a jar. Over time, watch it fill with blessings. This visual reminder will reinforce the habit and offer encouragement during moments of doubt.

3. **Incorporate Gratitude into Prayer:** When praying, take a few moments specifically to express your gratitude. Thank God for the blessings in your life and reflect on how they shape your spiritual journey. This practice invites divine connection and appreciation into your daily communication with God.

4. **Engage Your Senses:** Take a moment to reflect on the simple pleasures in life—the sound of laughter, the aroma of your favorite meal, or the feel of a loved one's embrace. Engaging your senses while expressing gratitude deepens your connection to these moments and enhances mindfulness.

5. **Set a Weekly Gratitude Review:** At the end of each week, review your entries. Notice patterns or recurring themes in your gratitude. This reflection will help you see how God is active in your life, filling you with renewed appreciation and strengthened faith.

6. **Share Your Gratitude:** Communicate your appreciation

to those around you. Share stories with friends and family about what you're thankful for. This practice not only uplifts your spirit but also encourages others to reflect on their blessings, creating a ripple effect of gratitude in your community.

By incorporating these methods into your daily routine, gratitude will become an inherent part of your spiritual journey. Over time, you'll discover that the practice of gratitude is a powerful act of faith—one that opens the door for deeper connection, trust, and acknowledgment of God's unfailing love.

As we conclude this subchapter, reflect on how the act of gratitude can have transformative effects on your faith journey. Recognize that small victories, shared experiences, and acknowledgments of blessings can propel you toward a more profound understanding of God's goodness. Gratitude can illuminate the path, guiding you through uncertainty and strengthening your trust in God's plan. In doing so, you embrace a practice that not only honors your faith but enriches every aspect of your life.

May your journey of daily gratitude enrich your faith and deepen your connection with God, bringing you closer to the heart of intentional living and spiritual growth. As you engage in these practices, let your gratitude flow from the well of trust within you, nourishing your spirit and nurturing your relationship with the divine.

Celebrating Life's Blessings

As we come to the end of our exploration into gratitude as a foundational element of faith, it is essential to recognize the significance of celebrating life's blessings—large and small. The act of celebrating is not merely about acknowledgment but is a profound expression of faith, a ritual that transcends the ordinary and invites us into a deeper relationship with God.

In our fast-paced world, where challenges can often overshadow moments of joy, taking the time to celebrate our blessings becomes a sacred practice. The stories we are about to explore are not just tales of triumph; they are windows into the heart of faith, revealing how gratitude serves as a bridge connecting us to each other and to God.

Consider the story of Sarah, a woman who faced significant trials during her journey. For years, she struggled with infertility, a burden that weighed heavily on her heart. Friends and family offered support, yet the desire for a child persisted like a whisper in her soul. During this difficult time, it would have been easy for Sarah to succumb to despair, to focus on her losses rather than her blessings. However, she made a conscious choice to seek gratitude amidst her struggles.

Every morning, she began a practice of gratitude journaling. At first, her entries were simple—she noted the kindness of a friend who brought over dinner or the beauty of a sunset that reminded her of God's creativity. Over time, Sarah found herself focusing less on what she lacked and more on the blessings surrounding her. This shift transformed her perspective and deepened her faith.

In her journey, Sarah found encouragement in the words of Scripture: "Every good and perfect gift is from above, coming down from the Father of the heavenly lights" (James 1:17). Holding onto this truth, she began celebrating even the smallest gifts. The ability to laugh with friends, the warmth of her family, and the moments of stillness became sacred memories woven into her tapestry of faith.

Months passed, and Sarah received the news she had longed for—she was pregnant! The day she discovered she was pregnant was not just a cause for joy; it represented a celebration of all the small victories along her journey. Surrounded by friends and family,

Sarah organized a celebration, not just for the baby but for the journey that led her to this moment.

With laughter and joy in the air, Sarah stood before her loved ones and shared her story. She talked about the moments that felt hopeless and the blessings she had celebrated along the way. The celebration was a testament not just to the gift of new life but to God's faithfulness throughout her journey. In expressing her gratitude, Sarah strengthened her community of believers, inviting them to reflect on their own blessings and share in the joy of her journey.

Much like the ripple effect of Sarah's celebration, let us consider the story of David, a young man who found himself navigating the precarious nature of life after college. Upon graduation, the weight of expectations pressed down on him. As both a son and a brother, David grappled with his responsibility to succeed in a competitive job market. The constant search for employment became a source of stress that overshadowed his ability to celebrate the milestones he had already accomplished.

To combat this overshadowing negativity, David turned to his faith. He began cultivating a habit of gratitude, writing down three things he was thankful for each day. Initially, he found it challenging. His days blurred into one another, and the struggle to find a job consumed him. Yet, he persisted. He started small: he celebrated the fact that he had graduated, he acknowledged the support of his family and friends, and he recognized his own resilience in a difficult landscape.

With time, David's heart began to shift. Rather than feeling burdened by unmet expectations, he started to celebrate what he had—the friendships that sustained him, the hope that fueled him, and the faith that guided his steps.

One evening, he attended a local faith gathering with friends, where the topic of gratitude surfaced. David felt compelled to share his journey. "You know," he began, "I spent a lot of time focusing on what I didn't have. I let my circumstances dictate my joy. But in choosing to celebrate my blessings—however small—I have discovered a joy that surpasses my circumstances."

His words resonated with many in the room. Others began to share their stories of struggle and victory. As they exchanged testimonials, a sense of community blossomed. David's simple act of celebrating his journey opened the door for others to reflect, share, and celebrate their blessings, no matter how small or significant.

Contrasting these stories with the narrative of Maya, an elderly woman from the community, shows us another dimension to the idea of celebrating life's blessings. Maya, known for her wisdom and kindness, understood the importance of gratitude. Having lived a long and fulfilling life, she had encountered her share of trials—loss, illness, and change. Yet, instead of becoming hardened by her experiences, Maya had cultivated an attitude of thanksgiving.

Each day, she would share her gratitude openly, encouraging those around her to recognize the beauty in the mundane. "Every day is a gift," she often said, "even in the trials of life." To celebrate her blessings, she initiated a monthly gathering in her home called "Gratitude Nights." Family and friends would gather to share meals, laughter, and, most importantly, their blessings from the past month.

During these gatherings, hearts would be filled through shared stories. Guests celebrated the birth of children, recoveries from illness, and even simple moments of nature that stirred their spirits. Maya believed that collectively sharing gratitude not only deepened their own faith but fostered a sense of belonging and community.

At one of these gatherings, Maya shared her reflection on Psalm 100:4, which states, "Enter his gates with thanksgiving and his courts with praise; give thanks to him and praise his name." Her exuberance filled the room as she invited everyone to enter into celebratory gratitude, emphasizing that praising God for His blessings creates a powerful, positive atmosphere where faith could thrive.

These heartfelt gatherings became a cherished tradition, serving as a reminder that our blessings are magnified when celebrated together. The shared faith among Maya's community fostered deeper connections, allowing individuals to encounter each other's journeys in vulnerability and authenticity.

As readers encounter these stories, it's essential to recognize the invitation to share our own experiences of gratitude. Each of us has a unique journey, woven with moments that reflect God's work in our lives. It is in sharing our testimonies that community is cultivated, faith is deepened, and blessings celebrated.

Take a moment to reflect: What are the blessings in your life? Consider both the big moments, like job promotions, births, and marriages, and the smaller ones—like a heartfelt conversation with a friend or the sunrise that graced your morning. Each blessing is an opportunity to celebrate and recognize God's hand over your life.

Imagine gathering with those you love, sharing stories, laughter, and gratitude. Perhaps you feel empowered to create your own "Gratitude Nights" or simply engage in sharing your blessings over a meal. Recognize that these moments not only uplift your spirit but contribute to a culture of gratitude—one that acknowledges the beauty of everyday life.

In small group settings, consider prompting discussions around gratitude. Invite members to share their recent blessings and how those moments affected their faith. Engage with questions that allow deeper reflection—how did recognizing a blessing in your life shift your perspective? What role does gratitude play in overcoming trials?

As we celebrate our individual and collective blessings, we also foster a deeper connection with God. Gratitude aligns our hearts with His goodness, reminding us of His faithfulness through every season. When we acknowledge our blessings, we simultaneously recognize the source—the One who gives abundantly, often in surprising ways.

Let us also consider the significance of routine in our recognitions of gratitude. Establishing personal rituals can help anchor our faith practices and ensure we celebrate each moment — whether it's through journaling, prayer, or planned gatherings.

Creating dedicated times for reflection allows us to pause amid the chaos of life and express our gratitude. In these sacred spaces, we can intentionally highlight our blessings, inviting the Holy Spirit to guide us in recognizing areas where God is at work.

This practice can transform our hearts, helping us navigate seasons of doubt or insecurity with a lens of appreciation. As Paul reminds us in Philippians 4:6-7, "Do not be anxious about anything, but in every situation, by prayer and petition, with thanksgiving, present your requests to God."

With gratitude as our framework, we can approach life's complexities rooted in faith. We begin to see that every trial brings the possibility of deeper growth, and each small victory is a testament to God's timing and presence in our lives.

As we close this exploration of gratitude and celebrate life's blessings, remember that every story shared, every blessing recognized, deepens not only our individual journeys but enriches the fabric of faith communities.

Invite others to join you on this adventure of faith, one where gratitude sets the stage for connection, transformation, and joy. By lifting our voices in celebration, we honor God's goodness, invite others in, and ultimately strengthen the bonds that tie our hearts and lives together in His love.

Take a moment after reading to reflect: what steps can you take today to celebrate your blessings? Consider sharing your thoughts with a friend, writing in a gratitude journal, or starting a group where blessings are honored and celebrated.

Together, as we recognize and celebrate the fullness of our lives, we unlock a sacred connection with God and each other, allowing our faith to grow and flourish in all its beauty and richness. Gratitude nurtures our connection with the divine, and by celebrating life's blessings, we embark on a journey that aligns our hearts with the heart of God.

Overcoming Doubt

Confronting Doubt

The sun dipped low in the sky, casting a warm golden hue over the horizon as the Skeptic sat on a worn bench in the local park. Jesse had always found solace in the whispers of nature, the rustling leaves, and the uncomfortable truth of silence. Although he adored moments like these, they often triggered a swell of thoughts, memories, and, more annoyingly, doubts—those persistent whispers that took root in his mind. They began as soft murmurs, subtle arguments that grew louder with each passing doubt: "What if this faith is all just a farce?" "What if there's something else out there, something more real?"

In his life, Jesse had wrestled with an internal conflict that often felt like an endless tug-of-war. On one side was a longing for belief—a desire to have faith that offered certainty, comfort, and community. On the other side loomed a darker, nagging voice, bolstered by experiences and observations that led him to question the very essence of existence. It was the voice of skepticism, an ever-present companion that had left him feeling isolated from the warmth of fellowship and the joy of unwavering faith.

Jesse could trace the origins of his doubts back to childhood. Growing up in a devout household had its advantages: he was surrounded by the stories of biblical heroes, taught the principles of love and grace, and encouraged to pray daily. But alongside those gentle teachings lay an implicit pressure—a weight of expectation that one must never question, never waver, and certainly never doubt. Such a fear-fueled belief system had, at times, felt suffocating.

He recalled sitting at the dinner table as his father passionately recounted the stories of Daniel in the lion's den, Jonah in the belly of a fish, and the miraculous feeding of thousands with a few loaves and fishes. Each tale was steeped in wonder and faith, but for young Jesse, they seeded something more: a skepticism that slowly snowballed into an insistent questioning as he grew older. "How can these stories be taken at face value?" he wondered. "What about the evidence? What about science?"

As his teenage years unfolded, he plunged deeper into books—philosophers, scientists, theologians, and even atheists—grappling with their arguments. The more he read, the more conflicted he became. Faith and skepticism danced a hazardous dance in his heart, often leading him to feel unworthy of spiritual expression. Jesse had longed to have a definitive answer, a miraculous transformation, a lightning bolt to dispel the haze of questioning and ambiguity.

It was at that moment, seated in the park, with the sun performing its slow descent, that he felt the weight of his doubt crushing down on him. "What must it feel like to truly believe?" he thought as he stared blankly ahead, watching children chase after one another, their laughter a contrast to the turmoil brewing inside him. "Is there really a God, and if so, why do I not feel His presence? Why can't I find that unwavering faith everyone speaks of?"

In a moment of vulnerability, Jesse reflected on the times when doubt had made itself known in tangible ways. There were nights spent in prayer, offering fervent requests but feeling only silence in return. There were weekends spent attending services where he sang songs of praise, yet deep inside, a part of him remained untouched and distant, like a spectator at a concert who never quite understood the music.

Struggling with his feelings of inadequacy, as if he were standing at the edge of a cliff, Jesse found it challenging to confront his doubts. Yet, in that moment of introspection, he recognized something profound: doubt was not the enemy. It was, in fact, an inevitable companion along the faith journey.

Scripture tells us that doubt exists, and it does not mean we are unworthy. In James 1:5, we read, "If any of you lacks wisdom, let him ask of God, who gives to all liberally and without reproach, and it will be given to him." In moments of confusion and uncertainty, we are invited to ask for help, to engage with our doubts honestly and bravely. The invitation is not to shy away but to confront those uncertainties head-on, leaning into the discomfort.

The very act of acknowledging doubt requires a level of vulnerability that many are unwilling to embrace. Acknowledgment creates an opportunity for growth—it opens the door to discovering new truths and perspectives. Jesse started to reflect not only on his struggles but also on the substances of faith he had engaged with: the warmth of other believers in moments of crisis, the quiet peace he had felt while praying even when the answers seemed far away, and the beauty of the world around him, where he saw God's fingerprints in nature itself.

Feeling emboldened amidst his reflections, he considered the biblical narrative of Thomas, often called "Doubting Thomas." After Christ's resurrection, it was Thomas who struggled to believe until he was given tangible proof. John 20:27 captures this moment vividly: "Then He said to Thomas, 'Put your finger here; see my hands. Reach out your hand and put it into my side. Stop doubting and believe.'" In this narrative, Jesus didn't scorn Thomas for his doubt; rather, he met him in it. That was true love—God inviting us closer despite our questions, instead of casting us aside. This insight began to shift Jesse's perspective; perhaps doubt could serve as a bridge rather than a barrier.

As he mulled over the interactions between doubt and faith, Jesse realized that it was inevitable that he would continue to encounter moments of disbelief. But how he navigated those moments could shape his faith significantly. What if he dared to see doubt as an opportunity to seek deeper understanding instead of an obstacle? What if questioning became a form of worship for him—one that paved the way for richer faith experiences?

Jesse understood that he needed to confront his doubts constructively, without dismissing them or allowing them to dominate his thoughts. It became essential for him to invite others into those moments of uncertainty, solidifying the idea that no one walks the faith journey alone. For too long, he had hidden behind a veil of isolation, thinking that doubt made him unworthy of companionship or understanding from other believers.

Summoning courage, he reached out to a friend from his church, Mia, who had often exuded an unshakeable faith. They met at a local café, the aroma of fresh coffee enveloping the space as they settled into a cozy booth. Jesse took a deep breath, feeling nervousness creep in. "Mia," he began, "I've been struggling, and I feel like I'm not where I should be in my faith. I doubt—so much."

Mia's eyes softened as she listened, and to Jesse's relief, her response was not judgmental but relatable. "You know," she said gently, "everyone doubts at some point. You're not alone. I doubt too, sometimes more than I care to admit."

Her honesty surprised him. Here was someone whose faith he admired, and yet she was willing to acknowledge her vulnerabilities. They spent the next hour sharing stories, discussing the moments when faith felt distant and how they both had navigated their doubts.

"I think it's important to embrace those questions," Mia reflected. "They can lead us to profound discoveries about God's nature and our own. Some of my doubts have drawn me closer to Scripture, and others have helped me understand myself better."

Listening to her made Jesse realize that the fears surrounding doubt often stemmed from the belief that faith should be absolute and unwavering. Yet faith, like any relationship, evolves and shifts as we grow. He began to see that struggle was not a sign of weakness but an essential part of faith—a testament to the willingness to wrestle with life, to seek out understanding, and to pursue growth.

As their conversation continued, Jesse grew emboldened. He felt lighter, as if shedding the heavy cloak of shame that had been wrapped around him for so long. He left the café that day with a strengthened resolve to not only acknowledge his doubts but to explore them further. He would study Scripture, read books on apologetics, and discuss his questions with others.

Doubt is not a dead end; it's a corridor, leading to deeper understandings and richer relationships. It's the very framework that offers room for faith to flourish, not merely exist. Jesse anticipated that such an approach might lead to painful realizations, moments of discomfort, and even fear—but it also held the promise of newfound clarity.

Still, the struggle would not end there. As he transitioned back to everyday life, Jesse encountered recurring doubts as they sprang up like weeds. A challenging conversation with a colleague about life's injustices struck a chord deep within him, leading to a whirlwind of thoughts: "How could a good God allow suffering?" "Can my faith withstand the harsh realities we see around us every day?"

In these moments, when doubt felt particularly potent, he turned to the Psalms. There was solace in diving into the cries of the psalmists—men and women who lamented their struggles and questioned God's presence. In Psalm 13:1-2, David cries out, "How long, O Lord? Will you forget me forever? How long will you hide your face from me? How long must I wrestle with my thoughts and day after day have sorrow in my heart?"

David's raw vulnerability echoed Jesse's own heart. Here was evidence that doubt, anger, and confusion could coexist with faith—a reminder that expressing his feelings to God was part of the journey. In those turbulent moments, as he grappled with questions, Jesse began to deliberately write them out in a journal, capturing his evolving thoughts and prayers. Each entry allowed him to articulate fears and uncertainties while inviting God into the discussion.

"I'm struggling to see you right now, God," he would write. "I don't understand your ways, and I feel lost."

Something changed as these words flowed onto the pages. By confronting his doubts through writing, Jesse began to feel less alone. It became a cathartic act, transforming the internal chaos into outward expressions. He found small bursts of inspiration as scripture illuminated the discussions he was having with himself: Romans 10:17 resonated clearly: "So faith comes from hearing, and hearing through the word of Christ."

Navigating doubt was not a linear path, but it became evident that wrestling with faith allowed him to build resilience in those challenging moments. He began leaning into community more, joining small groups where discussions on personal struggles were welcomed. It was refreshing to hear others share their own challenges, building a supportive environment where doubts were welcomed rather than shunned.

Jesse's faith journey metered on community and accountability. He learned to initiate conversations with fellow believers about their own doubts. They engaged in scripture readings, prayer, and personal reflection together, developing a richer understanding of faith grounded in vulnerability.

Each week he found himself more able to embrace uncertainty, viewing it through a lens of exploration rather than fear. Instead of shying away from difficult conversations or questions, he confronted them with courage. The emotional turmoil of doubting transformed into a readiness to immerse himself in learning, growing beside trusted friends and mentors who illuminated the path through shared experience.

The more Jesse confronted his doubts, the more he began to recognize the contour of his faith evolving. Embracing doubt allowed for a more profound authenticity in his spiritual life. He learned that faith expands when we lean into the unknown, allowing God to step into those areas of confusion and confusion.

Reflecting on his now deepened perspective, he was reminded of the shipwrecked apostle Paul, who clung to hope despite numerous trials. He read this poignant truth in Romans 5:3-4: "Not only that, but we rejoice in our sufferings, knowing that suffering produces endurance, and endurance produces character, and character produces hope."

Jesse's struggles with doubt became a mirrored reflection of his lifelong journey—teaching him that it was through the challenges of faith where growth often sprouted. Each time he uncovered a new layer of understanding, he welcomed it with gratitude. He began to express thankfulness for the questions he'd once feared, knowing that they helped ground him further in an honest relationship with God.

His faith hadn't exploded into perfect certainty; instead, it faithfully expanded through the messiness of doubt. The conflict within was still present, wrestling at times—but now it served as an indicator of his spiritual development and desire for growth. Jesse understood that faith was not just a mental exercise; it was a lived experience, one that included highs and lows, joy and anguish.

As the sun began to set that day, Jesse felt a sense of peace washing over him. Yes, doubts would return; they would ebb and flow like the tide. But he welcomed it; he stood at the edge, ready to dive in rather than retreat. As he rose from the park bench with renewed purpose, he vowed to rejoice in the tension of faith, learning to navigate the journey alongside his doubts, allowing them to draw him closer to God.

In those moments of uncertainty, he felt a newfound assurance—the assurance that he was not alone, that God stood with him in the struggles, welcoming each question, each wrestle, each tear. Here, in the beauty of faith and doubt intertwined, Jesse had found his path—a pathway of resilience, growth, and strength, all stemming from the willingness to confront what remained in shadow. And so, he walked forward, step by step, arm in arm, with faith and doubt entwined on a journey toward discovery.

Faith's Response to Doubt

In the journey of faith, doubt can often feel like an unwelcome companion. It surfaces in moments of uncertainty, whispers of skepticism, and a myriad of questions that can leave us feeling adrift. Yet, it's essential to recognize that doubt is not the opposite of faith; rather, it is often part of the journey within it. By examining biblical stories and personal testimonies, we can better understand faith's response to doubt. This exploration serves not only to shed light on how characters in scripture confronted their skepticism but also to offer encouragement to us as we navigate our doubts.

Take, for example, the story of Thomas, one of the twelve disciples. Known famously as "Doubting Thomas," he was absent when Jesus appeared to the other disciples after His resurrection. When they excitedly shared the news with him, Thomas responded with skepticism, declaring, "Unless I see the nail marks in his hands and put my finger where the nails were, and put my hand into his side, I will not believe it" (John 20:25 NIV). In this moment, we see a raw expression of doubt, one that many of us can relate to.

Thomas' need for tangible proof epitomizes the struggle many face when belief is challenged by doubt.

However, the story does not conclude with Thomas' doubt. Eight days later, Jesus appeared again, this time with Thomas present. He spoke directly to Thomas, inviting him to touch His wounds and no longer be faithless but believing. This moment of divine revelation was transformative for Thomas. He responded,

"My Lord and my God!" (John 20:28 NIV). This biblical account illustrates that faith's response to doubt can take many forms—through questioning, seeking, and ultimately, believing. Jesus' willingness to meet Thomas in his skepticism provides a model for how we might approach our doubts. Instead of shying away from them, we can invite God into our questioning.

Faith is an active response to the uncertainties we face. It doesn't deny the existence of doubt but rather acknowledges it as part of the searching journey toward deeper understanding. Personal testimonies often echo this sentiment. A friend, Sarah, once shared her story of battling profound doubt during a period of significant loss. Following the unexpected death of her father, she found herself questioning the very tenets of her faith. "I was angry, confused, and didn't know how to reconcile my grief with my belief in a loving God," she recounted.

In her struggle, Sarah did not suppress her doubts or ignore her anger. Instead, she leaned into her faith community, seeking understanding through both prayer and conversation. She began to engage deeply with scripture, exploring the Psalms where the authors frequently expressed feelings of despair, abandonment, and doubt. "Reading those scriptures allowed me to feel less alone," Sarah said. "It gave me room to wrestle with my feelings and know that I wasn't disqualified from faith just because I was struggling."

Sarah's experience mirrors the biblical pattern of doubt

addressed through faith. The Psalms, for instance, provide a rich tapestry of life's complexities, capturing the spectrum of human emotion. Psalm 13 offers a poignant example, where the psalmist cries out, "How long, O LORD? Will you forget me forever? How long will you hide your face from me?" (Psalm 13:1 NIV). This raw expression of doubt doesn't terminate in despair; instead, it transitions into a declaration of trust: "But I trust in your unfailing love; my heart rejoices in your salvation" (Psalm 13:5 NIV). Such passages serve as testimonies that faith can coexist with doubt, guiding us toward resolution and understanding.

As we reflect on our journeys with doubt, we may find ourselves asking how faith has guided us through challenging times. Consider moments when uncertainty threatened your belief. Did you turn to scripture, seek counsel from others, or cry out in prayer? These acts themselves are responses of faith—affirmations that, despite feelings of doubt, you are actively seeking connection with God.

Engaging in practices that address doubt can provide clarity and affirmation. Here are a few practical exercises designed to help readers confront and overcome their doubts:

1. **Journaling Doubts and Prayers**: Set aside time to write down your doubts and questions. Follow this by writing a prayer that directly addresses these feelings. Engaging with your fears in this manner can help you articulate them more clearly, often revealing underlying truths.

2. **Scripture Reflection**: Choose passages that deal with doubt and faith, such as Matthew 14:31, where Jesus says to Peter, "You of little faith, why did you doubt?" Reflect on these verses and consider how they apply to your own experiences. What encouragement do they offer?

3. **Seek Community**: Reach out to a trusted friend or

mentor and share your doubts. Engaging in honest conversation About your faith struggles can provide you with different perspectives and insights that often lead to resolution.

4. **Meditative Prayer**: Spend time in silence before God, inviting Him into your doubts. Sometimes, we learn the most in the stillness, where clarity can emerge from uncertainty.

5. **Explore the Psalms**: Select a Psalm reflecting doubt and read it slowly, allowing its words to resonate. Meditate on each line, considering it as a prayer that voices your feelings to God. Let this practice remind you that doubt has been woven into the fabric of faith long before your struggles began.

6. **Testimony Sharing**: Create a space, whether in a small group or with friends, where people can share their stories of doubt and faith. Listening to others' journeys can inspire and remind you that you are not alone in your struggles.

Faith's response to doubt is an invitation to explore the depth of our beliefs more thoroughly. Doubt can provoke a search for truth that leads to genuine faith. The journey doesn't end with a definitive answer; rather, it often deepens the relationship we have with God. We see this in the life of the prophet Habakkuk, who voiced his doubts openly, wrestling with questions about God's justice amidst suffering. Yet, by the end of the book, Habakkuk's conclusion is a powerful affirmation of faith: "Yet I will rejoice in the LORD, I will be joyful in God my Savior" (Habakkuk 3:18 NIV). His doubts led to a deeper understanding of faith.

Let us also consider the story of Gideon. When called by God to save Israel from oppression, Gideon voiced skepticism about his abilities and God's promise. He requested multiple signs from God, laying down a fleece to verify the divine assurance he had received.

God patiently responded, affirming Gideon's call despite his doubt. Here, we see that faith often welcomes questions and seeks signs of assurance. God does not chastise Gideon for his uncertainty; instead, He accommodates it and provides reassurance.

This narrative encourages readers to remember that God values sincerity in our doubts and questions. When we approach Him authentically, God meets us where we are, guiding us to a place of stronger faith. In times of doubt, may we follow Gideon's example and do the brave work of seeking truth, developing our understanding of God's character and promises.

As we navigate doubt, it's crucial to remember that faith doesn't expect us to have all the answers or to remain unshakeable in the face of questions. Recognizing that doubt can strengthen faith transforms it from an adversary into a profound teacher. Reflections on past experiences can often reveal growth and resilience that doubt prompted.

Consider the early church faced with tribulation. The Apostle Paul experienced doubt, fear, and anguish throughout his ministry, as evidenced in his letters. Yet, he consistently turned back to faith. In 2 Corinthians 12:10, he declares, "For when I am weak, then I am strong." This paradox highlights how faith can shine brightly amid doubt, illuminating a pathway through struggles and uncertainties.

To reinforce these lessons, engage in reflective journaling to consider how God has been faithful in your life. Record instances where doubt led you to a deeper understanding or where, through questioning, you clarified your beliefs. This practice not only solidifies your experiences but serves as a testament to growth.

Our faith can flourish amidst doubt when we adopt a posture of curiosity rather than fear. Questions, when approached with humility and integrity, hold the potential to lead us closer to God. What was a doubt that once troubled you, yet now serves as a testimony? Perhaps a situation that once seemed insurmountable now speaks to your journey's transformative nature, reminding you of God's faithfulness.

In closing, embrace doubt as a part of your faith journey. Acknowledge it as an invitation to explore the depths of your belief, lean into relationships within your faith community, and seek God earnestly through prayer and scripture. As you confront and process doubt, remember the biblical narratives that assure you—faith does not dismiss doubt but engages it. Ultimately, allow your struggles with doubt to serve as stepping stones towards a deeper, richer faith, transforming the inquiry of your heart into a more profound connection with God. May every question lead you closer to the truth, and may every moment of doubt culminate in a celebration of faith renewed.

Building Resilience in Faith

In the journey of faith, doubt often emerges as an inevitable companion, challenging our beliefs and shaking the foundations of our trust in God. Yet, amidst those shadows of uncertainty, stories of resilience shine brightly, illuminating the path toward spiritual strength. This subchapter will explore the essence of building resilience in faith through the lens of individuals who have faced skepticism and emerged transformed and empowered. As we delve into their narratives, we will celebrate growth, reflect on obstacles, and equip ourselves with actionable steps to foster resilience when faced with doubt.

Consider the story of Sarah, a woman who grew up in a faith-filled environment but found herself grappling with existential questions as she entered adulthood. With a college education, she encountered diverse worldviews that challenged her long-held beliefs. Skepticism crept in like an uninvited guest, prompting her to question the very core of her faith. Late-night discussions with friends led to a chasm of doubt that seemed impossible to bridge. Feeling lost, Sarah turned to prayer, seeking clarity and understanding from God, yet, like many, she struggled with silence and unanswered questions.

However, it was in the depths of her doubt that Sarah discovered an unexpected strength. Embracing her skepticism rather than shunning it, she decided to embark on a journey of exploration. Sarah delved into scripture and sought guidance from trusted mentors, using her doubts as a springboard for deeper understanding. Her journey wasn't without its challenges; moments of frustration and confusion would arise, yet each time she would circle back to God in prayer, daring to express her uncertainties. It was in this vulnerability that Sarah found resilience. She learned that doubt didn't define her faith; rather, it became a catalyst for growth.

Through her struggles, Sarah met others who had traversed similar paths, individuals who had faced their own doubts and emerged on the other side with a deeper, more vibrant faith. Inspired by their stories, she cultivated a community of believers who shared their experiences, reinforcing the idea that the journey of faith is often marked by ups and downs. In these relationships, Sarah found not only encouragement but also accountability, which bolstered her own resolve.

In sharing her newfound understanding of resilience with others, Sarah emphasized that faith isn't about eliminating doubt but navigating it with grace. She encouraged friends struggling with their own uncertainties, inviting them to see doubts not as barriers but as bridges to deeper truths. Her story radiated hope because it exemplified the transformative power of community, vulnerability, and faith. Through her journey, she learned to embrace the complexity of faith, realizing that it was through her darkest moments that the light of her trust in God shone the brightest.

Another powerful narrative is that of Mark, a dedicated church leader whose faith was put to the test in a most profound way. When unexpected tragedy struck his family, Mark found himself grappling with anger and confusion, questioning God's goodness amidst his sorrow. The cultural narrative whispers that faith should protect us from life's challenges, yet Mark discovered the harsh reality that pain is often a part of the human experience—faithfulness does not exempt one from suffering.

In the days following his loss, Mark felt the weight of doubt like never before. Initially, he was hesitant to express his feelings of skepticism to others for fear of being misunderstood or judged. However, in the quiet of his grief, he found solace in honest prayer. He poured out his heart to God, unfiltered and raw, wrestling with frustration and longing for clarity. This act of vulnerability was transformative; by opening his heart to God, he forged a deeper connection even amid his pain.

Through his mourning, Mark learned the importance of resilience rooted in faith. He shared these revelations with his congregation, candidly recounting his struggles. Instead of presenting a polished image of unwavering faith, Mark chose to reveal his authentic journey through doubt and despair. His transparency invited others to acknowledge their own struggles, fostering an environment in which doubt could be acknowledged and discussed openly. This communal acknowledgment created a safe space where individuals were free to explore their own questions, doubts, and faith.

Mark's story exemplified that resilience in faith often entails confronting discomfort, not avoiding it. Through his trials, he cultivated empathy and understanding, enabling him to support others in their journeys of doubt. As he walked alongside those facing their own crises of faith, Mark learned that vulnerability can be a powerful vehicle for facilitating healing and growth within a community. The resilience he nurtured became contagious, inspiring others to embrace their doubts as part of their faith journey.

Resilience also flourished in characters like Aisha, a young woman who felt the sting of rejection when her church community reacted harshly to her honest doubts about their doctrines. Feeling isolated, she wrestled with feelings of shame and confusion, questioning if she truly belonged in faith spaces. The rejection cut deep, yet Aisha refused to let it extinguish her search for truth. Instead, she turned to God's word, seeking affirmation of her worth and significance.

A pivotal moment came when Aisha sought solace in outreach programs, serving those who struggled with their faith in tangible ways. It was there that she encountered people who had faced similar rejections, individuals whose journeys of doubt mirrored her own. As she engaged with this diverse group, Aisha began to realize that the bonds of community could arise even in the face of skepticism.

Through her experiences, Aisha learned the transformative power of resilience; she discovered that embracing her doubts could lead to strength and compassion. She began sharing her story and advocating for a supportive environment where others felt comfortable exploring their faith questions without fear of judgment. As Aisha embraced her own journey of doubt, she encouraged others to cultivate resilience by affirming that doubt is a shared human experience.

Now that we've reflected on the stories of Sarah, Mark, and Aisha, it's crucial to understand that building resilience in faith is not merely about overcoming doubt but transforming it into an integral part of one's spiritual growth. To foster resilience, individuals can adopt several practical steps:

First, cultivate a habit of open dialogue about doubt. Connecting with others allows for shared experiences that promote mutual understanding. This requires creating a community where questioning is welcomed and discussions are encouraged. Honest conversations can forge deeper relationships, reinforcing an awareness that we are not alone in our struggles.

Second, engage regularly in reflective practices such as journaling. This allows for personal exploration and clarity about feelings of doubt. Writing can serve as an outlet for frustrations and uncertainties, and revisiting these reflections can illuminate spiritual growth over time.

Third, study scripture not just for answers, but to find companionship in the narratives of doubt. Many biblical figures wrestled with uncertainty, and their experiences can provide comfort. Delving into their stories can reveal that doubt is often part of the faith journey, offering practical insights into navigating one's own struggles. Consider journaling about what you find in Biblical accounts of doubt; identify themes that resonate with your experiences.

Fourth, embrace vulnerability in prayer. Pour out your heart to God, allowing authenticity to seep into your communication with Him. This act of vulnerability fosters deeper trust, inviting God into your questions and uncertainties. Remember, God already knows your doubts; laying them bare before Him may help you feel a connection in your struggle.

Fifth, engage in acts of service to others who may be facing their own doubts. Supporting those in need fosters an environment of compassion and resilience. By walking alongside others, we can understand the community's strength while building confidence in our convictions.

Finally, practice patience with yourself and others. Developing resilience takes time; the journey through doubt is not linear. Embrace the ups and downs as part of the growth process, shifting your perspective toward a mindset of gradual progress.

As readers reflect on these actionable steps, it is crucial to recognize that building resilience in faith is an ongoing process. The stories of Sarah, Mark, and Aisha remind us that doubt can serve as a pathway to deeper intimacy with God. With each struggle we face, we have an opportunity to fortify our foundation of faith, transforming skepticism into strength.

We conclude this journey with an invitation to celebrate growth through doubt. Each person's path is unique, yet we collectively face the trials of faith. Acknowledge the strength drawn from your experiences and the lessons learned throughout your journey.

Reflect on how overcoming obstacles and uncertainties has deepened your faith, recognizing that resilience is born in the tension between doubt and trust.

As you move forward, remember that every doubt acknowledged is an opportunity for growth—a chance to embrace the complexities of faith. Lean into your community, explore your questions, and engage in meaningful prayer. Together, let us continue building resilience in our faith journeys, confronting doubt with courage and strength. In doing so, we create spaces where faith becomes a living, breathing testimony of hope and resilience, even amid uncertainty. Allow your journey of faith to be a source of inspiration for others, illuminating the path toward authentic, resilient belief.

The Journey of Faith

Understanding Faith as a Journey

Faith is often perceived as a destination—a fixed point we strive to reach, a summit where doubts are silenced and answers are clear. This perception can create an illusion that faith is an event we can check off our lists, much like attending a seminar or crossing a landmark off a bucket list. However, true faith is not defined by a single moment of clarity or realization; rather, it is a continuous journey filled with twists, turns, valleys, and peaks. Each person's journey is unique, yet woven together with threads of solidarity, shared experiences, and collective learning.

As we explore the concept of faith as a journey, it's fitting to consider the various characters who inhabit the pages of this narrative—each with their own struggles, breakthroughs, and evolving understanding of what it means to trust in God. Their stories reflect the universal quest for purpose and meaning, encouraging readers to recognize that every journey is significant and interconnected with one another's. In doing so, we invite you to embrace your own path, embracing both challenges and triumphs, knowing they contribute to your growth and understanding.

Let us begin by walking in the shoes of the Woman at the Well, whose transformative encounter with Jesus serves as a poignant reminder of the individual nature of faith journeys. Initially burdened by her past, she approached the well carrying not just a water jar, but a lifetime of shame, guilt, and societal judgment. It is easy to imagine the internal turmoil as she weighed her worth against the expectations of those around her. This moment at the well marks the beginning of her journey—a departure from concealment and fear toward embrace and acceptance.

Jesus offers her living water, symbolizing the life that can only be found in a relationship with Him. This pivotal encounter illustrates that a significant part of faith is the willingness to let go of preconceived notions about ourselves and allow God's truth to redefine our identities. As her story unfolds, the reader observes her evolution from uncertainty to boldness. She becomes a vessel of hope for her community, sharing her newfound faith with others. This journey teaches us that faith is not merely about receiving but also about sharing, impacting others in profound ways.

Now, let us reflect on the experiences of the Skeptic, whose journey is characterized by a different set of challenges. Often questioning and analyzing his beliefs, he grapples with doubt in a way that is all too familiar for many. His narrative provides insights into the struggles that come with uncertainty, showcasing that questions are a vital part of any faith journey. The Skeptic ventures into the unknown, wrestling with uncertainties that can either engulf him in despair or propel him toward deeper understanding. His inquiry is not a sign of weakness, but rather an invitation to explore the very essence of faith: trust in what we cannot see.

Through various encounters—be it through meaningful discussions with others or quiet reflections in solitude—the Skeptic begins to discover that questions can lead to deeper revelations. Just like the Woman at the Well, he learns that vulnerability and honesty in his inquiries open the door for growth. By articulating his challenges rather than suppressing them, he creates a fertile ground for faith to flourish. This journey highlights the importance of allowing doubts to coexist with faith, ultimately enhancing one's relationship with God.

Both the Woman at the Well and the Skeptic personify the essential truth that faith is dynamic—it grows and evolves as we navigate life's complexities. Their journeys unfold against the backdrop of community; their stories intertwine with those of others who walk alongside them. The Encourager, for instance, finds strength in the stories of his peers, witnessing how collective experiences weave into the fabric of his faith. He learns that community amplifies individual journeys, fostering connections that enrich and deepen his understanding of trust in God.

The Encourager's path reflects the idea that faith is not meant to be cultivated in isolation. Instead, it thrives within the context of relationships and shared experiences. He recognizes that every individual brings a unique perspective, contributing to the broader narrative of faith that resonates through generations. By engaging with others, the Encourager discovers transformative power in unity; he experiences firsthand the power of encouragement, support, and shared vulnerability. This realization invites readers to seek fellowship where they can share their own journeys, celebrating the collective growth that emerges from unity.

As each character's journey unfolds, we find commonalities in their stories that reveal the essence of faith as the journey rather than the destination. Their experiences teach us that growth often arises from challenges—those moments of doubt, the turbulence of life, and the heartaches that shape us. It is through adversity that we often uncover profound revelations about ourselves and God. As we embrace our own journeys, we must ask ourselves: What challenges have shaped my faith? How have these experiences led me toward a deeper understanding of God's presence in my life?

To foster deeper introspection, let us pause and reflect on the following questions:

1. When I think about my faith journey, what milestones stand out to me?

2. How have my challenges shaped my perspectives on faith and trust in God?

3. Are there moments when I have struggled with doubt? How

did I navigate those feelings?

4. In what ways have I experienced growth through adversity?

5. How has the support of others influenced my faith journey, and how can I offer support to those around me?

These reflective questions are not merely prompts; they serve as invitations to engage with your faith story actively. Journaling your responses allows you to articulate your journey and observe the threads that connect your experiences to those of others. Through writing, you can gain clarity on how your path has shaped your understanding. Embrace the opportunity to celebrate your milestones, be they small victories or significant turning points.

As we continue to explore the interconnectedness of our faith journeys, consider the Muslim phrase "Insha'Allah"—translated as "If God wills." It reflects an acknowledgment that our lives are part of a larger narrative governed by divine will. Likewise, embracing the notion that our paths are divinely orchestrated can provide a sense of peace amidst life's uncertainties. It invites us to practice patience as we navigate the landscape of our faith journeys, trusting that God is present even when we cannot see the bigger picture.

The theme of patience resonates deeply throughout the broader context of our book. Just as seasons change, so too do our spiritual seasons. Whether we find ourselves in a period of blossoming growth or in a winter of struggle, each season contributes to our journey. The encouraging notion, however, lies in the promise of renewal. Just as nature reveals cycles of life, our faith also experiences cycles of discovery, learning, and growth.

Pause for a moment and consider the beauty found in the diversity of faith journeys. We each bring unique experiences, backgrounds, and lessons learned along the way that enrich the canvas of faith. The woman from the well, the skeptic, and the encourager—all different yet all part of the same human experience.

Together, they remind us that faith is a shared journey, a collective pilgrimage where each voice contributes to the overarching narrative.

As we conclude this exploration of faith as a journey, embrace the idea that your story matters. The lessons learned, the struggles faced, and the triumphs celebrated all carry significance in the larger tapestry of faith. Just as each character learns through their encounters, so too are you invited to learn through your experiences—a continuous unfolding of purpose and understanding.

Let us remember that as we navigate our paths, we must not measure success by a singular destination but by the authenticity of our journeys. There is profound beauty in the ongoing quest for understanding, in the unspoken moments of vulnerability, and the lives intertwined with ours. In recognizing that faith is a journey, we create space for growth, transformation, and connection—each experience a stepping stone that propels us closer to understanding the heart of God.

In the days and years to come, may we all choose to embrace our journeys with courage and openness, celebrate our individual and communal paths, and seek to uplift one another as we walk together in faith. We invite you to pick up your pen and begin journaling—documenting your own journey, reflecting on your experiences, and envisioning the incredible ways God will continue to weave your story within His greater narrative. Accept this invitation to journey deeper, for each step is a testament to your faith.

Milestones of Faith

In the vast tapestry of faith, each person's journey weaves a unique story, filled with vibrant threads of hope, struggle, and triumph. As we embark on a deeper exploration of milestones of faith, we find ourselves not merely chronicling episodes but recognizing transformational moments that serve as signposts along our spiritual paths. These moments create indelible shifts in our perspectives and attitudes, urging us to grow and reflect on our connections with God and each other.

Consider Sarah, a devoted mother, who found her faith tested during a tumultuous season of her life. Working tirelessly to support her family, she often felt overwhelmed by the weight of responsibilities. The demands of nurturing her children while balancing a full-time job left little room for self-care, and her spiritual practice began to wane. One day, while driving home from work, she felt an undeniable pull to stop at a small chapel she had passed many times but never entered. The chapel loomed on the corner, its simplicity calling out amidst the chaos of her life.

As she pushed open the door, a wave of peace engulfed her. The dimly lit space was adorned with candles flickering gently, casting a warm glow that seemed to embrace her weary soul. Sarah knelt before the altar, her heart heavy with a mixture of exhaustion and desperation. It was here, in these sacred moments of vulnerability, that she poured out her fears and burdens to God, realizing how crucial it was to seek Him amid life's storms.

This encounter became a pivotal milestone for Sarah. She emerged from the chapel with a renewed sense of purpose, committing to carve out time each week to reconnect with her faith, prioritize prayer, and attend a women's Bible study group. Reflecting on this experience, Sarah recognized that stepping inside the chapel wasn't about the physical act alone; it was about her willingness to seek rest for her soul, marking the beginning of a deeper communion with God.

Like Sarah, many individuals experience moments of awakening that alter their spiritual trajectory. These milestones often manifest in varied forms — a heartbreaking loss, an unexpected blessing, a conversation with a stranger, or a quiet moment of revelation. They are not always grand or dramatic; sometimes, they're quiet transformations that occur within the heart.

Think of Mark, who wrestled with doubt throughout his teenage years. Raised in a Christian home, he often found himself questioning the very foundation of his beliefs. The world felt vast and confusing, and he struggled to align his faith with the questions that echoed in his mind. One night, during a youth retreat, he felt moved to share his struggles with the group. As he spoke, he watched as others nodded in understanding, revealing that he was not alone in his doubts.

That night, the milestone for Mark was not merely the act of sharing but the realization that vulnerability is a vital aspect of faith. His courage to express his uncertainties allowed him to foster genuine connections with others, encouraging a dialogue among peers that dispelled loneliness. Subsequently, the discussions that followed not only enriched his understanding but also bolstered his faith, transforming doubt into deeper inquiry and engagement.

Mark's journey highlights the significance of community within the faith journey. Each milestone shared encourages connections and fosters collective growth. It reminds us that we are not solitary travelers but part of a larger spiritual family, where each person's journey influences the others. The courageous act of speaking out can inspire others to reveal their struggles and triumphs, creating an environment of support and understanding.

Faith journeys also often lead us through valleys of despair, where milestones of renewal can emerge unexpectedly. Take, for example, Laura, a woman who faced the heartbreaking loss of her father to illness. In the depths of her sorrow, she felt isolated and angry, struggling to reconcile her faith with the stark reality of loss.

Yet, a few weeks later, in the midst of her grief, she joined a grief support group at her church. It was there that Laura began to share her feelings, revealing her pain and how it affected her relationship with God.

As she engaged with others who understood her struggle, Laura started to notice shifts within herself. The act of allowing others to enter into her pain and share theirs opened a pathway to healing. Her milestone came in the form of understanding that grief and faith could coexist. It became an opportunity for her to experience God's comfort in ways she had previously overlooked. Through prayer, deep conversations, and reflection, Laura realized that her sorrow was a part of her faith journey, leading her closer to God rather than pushing her away.

Reflecting upon these milestones encourages readers to recognize the moments in their own lives that have forged their faith. Each journey is a mosaic, composed of experiences that may seem small or insignificant but collectively shape our understanding of God and ourselves. These life events whisper reminders that our pursuit of faith is a process, not a destination.

In the same way, milestones can manifest as acts of service. Consider David, a retired teacher who felt a stirring in his heart to give back to his community. At first, he wondered if he had anything to offer, feeling inadequate as he left his teaching career behind. But a conversation with a friend who volunteered at a local shelter ignited a spark within him. The friend encouraged David to share his love for learning with children who needed mentorship. Taking a leap of faith, David offered to volunteer as a reading tutor, and soon, he found himself immersed in the lives of children whose thirst for knowledge reignited his own passion.

This volunteering experience became a milestone for David, marking a period of rejuvenation in his faith journey. It reminded him that serving others is a natural extension of faith, breathing life into the commandment to love our neighbors. As he dedicated his time to mentoring young minds, he discovered that faith flourishes in the act of giving. Each child inspired him, reigniting his joy and purpose as he witnessed the impact of his support. David learned that milestones aren't solely about individual achievements; they often involve uplifting and nurturing those around us.

As we explore the stories of these characters, we invite readers to recognize the beauty in their own faith milestones. Whether it's an encounter that deepened understanding, a moment of vulnerability, a choice to serve others, or a hard-won lesson from loss, each milestone is an essential part of the journey. They serve to remind us to celebrate our individual stories—the moments that seem minor yet contribute profoundly to our overall growth.

Milestones can also encourage us to acknowledge the more subtle changes that take place within. For instance, reflect on Rachel, a once-anxious individual who struggled with habitual worry. Through a newfound commitment to prayer and gratitude, she slowly began to shift her mindset. What started as a conscious effort to turn her worries into prayers became a transformative practice, allowing her to cultivate peace in her life. This gradual transition became her milestone, as she discovered the power of trusting God with her anxieties, ultimately revealing new heights of faith.

Milestones of faith, however small or significant, invite us to reflect on our trajectories. Deep reflection can help solidify lessons learned through trials and victories. They remind us that faith is not static but evolves as we navigate life's diverse landscape. We can trace how experiences build upon one another, enriching our understanding, shaping our responses, and deepening our connection with God.

As we explore our own spiritual milestones, it's crucial to take a moment to consider the span of our journeys—what has shaped our faith? Have we experienced moments of questioning or doubt? Have challenges led to discoveries of new depths of trust? Journaling can serve as a powerful tool in this process. By putting pen to paper, we gain clarity and insight. It allows us to chart our journeys and note the pivotal moments, creating a narrative tapestry of our faith experiences.

We might ask ourselves, What was a pivotal moment when I felt God's presence most profoundly? Was there an experience that shifted my perspective or understanding of faith? How has my community shaped or influenced my journey? Taking the time to reflect on such questions can foster a sense of accomplishment as we recognize growth and transformation over time.

Now, perhaps, you've been inspired by the stories of Sarah, Mark, Laura, David, and Rachel. Each life embodies different aspects of faith and distinct milestones that connect to the universal human experience. They remind us that every step we take in faith is meaningful—whether it's in moments of clarity and joy or in valleys of sorrow and uncertainty. Celebrating both the grand and the quiet milestones emboldens our spirits and aligns our hearts with God's design for our lives.

As we conclude this exploration of milestones within our faith journeys, let's take a moment to pause, breathe, and reflect. Think of a milestone—perhaps a moment of transformation, a challenge turned into triumph, or a relationship that deepened your understanding of God. Consider how it has influenced your path and what it still teaches you.

Invite gratitude into your reflections. Acknowledge how far you have come, not just from the destination but simply in your willingness to walk the road of faith. Each step, no matter how small, contributes to the beautiful picture of your spiritual life.

The journey of faith is rich with experiences. When we honor our milestones, we celebrate our stories and recognize the active presence of God in our lives. May you continue to embrace the journey, honoring your milestones and allowing them to propel you forward with faith, hope, and love.

The Community of Faith Journeys

The tapestry of faith is often woven from the threads of individual experiences, but it is in community that these threads find strength and beauty. Every believer's journey is unique—a story filled with triumphs, struggles, doubts, and epiphanies. Yet, when these personal odysseys are shared within a community, something transformative happens. Walls of isolation crumble, and in their place, bridges of understanding and support arise. This subchapter seeks to explore the richness of shared faith journeys, emphasizing the fundamental truth that our paths shine brighter when illuminated by the shared light of others.

The Encourager recalls a moment during a particularly challenging season in their life when their faith community came together in an extraordinary way. It was a time when the world felt heavy, and fear loomed large like a dark cloud. The Encourager had recently lost a family member, sending shockwaves of grief through their life. Despite the personal turmoil, they were not alone. As the news spread through their church community, something remarkable unfolded: the community enveloped them in love and support, demonstrating the tangible embodiment of faith in action.

In one of the most poignant memories, members of the church organized a meal train—a simple yet powerful initiative where volunteers signed up to deliver meals to the Encourager's home. With each meal that arrived, not only did they find nourishment for their body, but also an outpouring of care that fed their spirit. Each visit came accompanied by heartfelt conversations, stories shared, and prayers lifted. This collective response of love and compassion was a balm for the Encourager's soul, teaching them the true essence of being part of a faith community.

It isn't just the grand gestures that make these communities special; it's the everyday moments of connection that build the fabric of support. The Encourager remembers gathering with friends for weekly Bible study—a cherished time where laughter mixed with tears and revelations danced amidst shared scriptures. It was during these intimate gatherings that individuals opened their hearts, sharing their doubts and fears alongside their joys and triumphs. They created a sacred space where vulnerability found acceptance, allowing everyone to be themselves without the pressure of perfection.

Through their stories, the Encourager learned that challenges aren't merely obstacles; they can serve as powerful catalysts for growth. One individual shared an experience of getting laid off, a moment that initially felt like the end of a journey. Yet, with communal support, they discovered new paths and opportunities they had not considered before. The encouragement to view setbacks as sacred pauses rather than dead ends created an atmosphere of hope and resilience. Each shared testimony was a reminder that faith can thrive even in uncertainty when tethered to a community that believes in you.

Faith journeys can also illuminate the paths of others. Every story shared, every lesson learned, brings inspiration to those listening. The Encourager recounted a powerful experience at a church retreat. One evening, they gathered around a crackling campfire, each sharing their faith journey. As stories unfolded, the air was thick with emotion—laughter mingled with tears, and each narrative created a rich tapestry of shared understanding. One story stood out: a member spoke openly about struggling with long-term addiction and the road to recovery. Their courage sparked a deep conversation that continued late into the night about vulnerability, healing, and the transformative power of grace.

As individuals shared, they recognized that they were not alone in their struggles. Their stories echoed similar experiences, revealing how shared pain can unite for healing. In a world inundated with messages of isolation and self-reliance, these shared moments reminded attendees of the healing power of faith lived out in community. It became evident that faith is not only a personal journey, but it is also meant to be a shared pilgrimage, one that can guide and uplift others along the way.

Through the years, the Encourager witnessed how collective journeys fortified relationships within their community. When one member faced a health crisis, others quickly rallied to offer support. Visits to the hospital, shared prayers, and the simple act of being present created an unbreakable bond, infusing faith within a shared purpose. This gave rise to a sense of belonging, assuring everyone that they were in this together. The struggles of one became the struggles of all, and in moments of collective anguish, love flourished.

As members navigated life's milestones together—births, graduations, marriages, and even losses—these moments etched themselves into the heart of the community. The Encourager learned that community isn't merely a backdrop for faith; it is an active participant, one that shapes individual narratives and creates new chapters in the story of faith.

Yet, as powerful as these shared experiences are, they also serve as a reminder of the responsibility each member bears within the community. The Encourager poses a reflective question to the readers: What role do you play in your faith community? How can your unique experiences contribute to fostering an environment that supports the collective journey?

It's essential to recognize that being an active participant means being mindful of how one engages with others. Encouraging words, shared meals, or simply being a listening ear can significantly impact someone on their faith journey. The Encourager emphasizes the importance of authenticity within these connections. By sharing honestly about one's own journey, the community becomes a place where others feel safe to unveil their struggles.

In considering their own role, the Encourager invites readers to reflect on moments when they were uplifted by others and encourages them to think about ways they can reciprocate that love and support. By being intentional, readers can create a ripple effect of encouragement, fostering a culture of trust and vulnerability that enhances the communal journey.

The Encourager also acknowledges that sometimes individuals may find it challenging to connect, perhaps due to personal circumstances or past experiences. This is where grace becomes essential. Understanding that everyone is at a different point in their journey allows the community to embrace diversity and foster inclusivity. It is imperative to approach these differences with open hearts and minds, recognizing that every story adds to the beautiful tapestry of the collective journey.

To enhance this sense of community, the Encourager suggests practical steps readers can take in their faith journeys. One vital step is to engage in open conversations with fellow community members. Sharing personal testimonies, no matter how painful, offers a launching pad for deeper discussions. It creates space for authentic connections to flourish, which in turn strengthens the fabric of support.

Another aspect that often binds communities is service. Engaging in outreach—whether through local ministries or helping a neighbor in need—embeds purpose into the collective journey. The Encourager recalls a service project that focused on revitalizing a local school. Participation in this endeavor sparked camaraderie and fueled inspiration among community members, reiterating how faith is manifested through action.

Additionally, the Encourager suggests forming small groups aimed at fostering deeper connections. These gatherings can provide intentional opportunities for individuals to come together regularly, share their journeys, and offer support. In these intimate settings, deeper conversations arise, allowing members to navigate their faith struggles alongside one another.

As the Encourager reflects on the importance of community, they share a particularly touching memory of their congregation coming together for a member faced with a terminal illness. It was a time marked by heavy hearts, yet the strength of their collective faith shone brightly. Each member contributed to a life celebration, sharing stories, creating a scrapbook of memories, and surrounding this precious member with love and encouragement until the very end. It was a powerful testament to the bond forged in love, highlighting the divine intersection of faith and community.

At the heart of these journeys lies the promise of belonging. It is the profound assurance that within the community, anyone can experience acceptance, love, and understanding. The Encourager encourages readers to recognize their own need for belonging, inviting them to contribute to creating a culture that champions inclusion and nurtures everyone's faith journey.

As this subchapter draws to a close, the Encourager invites readers to reflect on the transformation that happens when faith is shared. It reminds them that every journey contributes to the collective story. Through shared experiences—both triumph and tragedy—everyone can foster a community that uplifts, supports, and strengthens faith.

Faith is meant to flourish in community, and by embracing shared journeys, individuals illuminate the path for one another. Readers are called to live out the beauty of their own narratives while simultaneously weaving them into the larger fabric of communal faith. May they step forward, embracing their roles within their faith communities, and remember that in the journey of faith, they are never truly alone. As they navigate the landscapes of faith, let them do so together, supporting one another on the beautiful journey ahead.

Celebrating Small Victories

The Power of Small Wins

In the intricate tapestry of faith, small victories often go unnoticed against the backdrop of grand narratives and overwhelming challenges. Yet, it is these seemingly insignificant triumphs that have the power to cultivate spiritual growth, inspire resilience, and foster joy. As we traverse our unique journeys of faith, it becomes paramount to recognize and celebrate these moments of achievement, no matter how small they may appear.

Consider the story of Sara, a busy mother of three, who found herself caught in the whirlwind of daily responsibilities. Between managing her career, caring for her children, and running the household, Sara often felt overwhelmed. In her quest for spiritual growth, she longed to carve out time for prayer and reflection, but the chaos of her life made it seem impossible. One particularly challenging week, after several failed attempts to establish a daily prayer routine, Sara finally managed to set aside just ten minutes each morning to sit quietly with her thoughts and offer up her prayers. Though this was just a small increment of time in the grand scheme of her day, the impact was profound.

Embracing that ten-minute commitment transformed Sara's mornings. It became a sacred space where she could connect with God and seek His guidance. The clarity that followed those brief moments of solitude carried her through the chaos of her day, rejuvenating her spirit and enhancing her ability to face challenges with grace. By choosing to honor that small victory, Sara opened the door to more significant moments of spiritual connection and growth.

Similarly, consider Michael, a college student grappling with doubt and anxiety in his faith journey. He struggled with trusting

God in the face of academic pressures and social expectations, often feeling isolated and burdened by his uncertainties. One evening, feeling particularly overwhelmed, he decided to engage in a simple act: he reached out to a fellow student about starting a prayer group. It was a small step—simply a conversation and an invitation—but it sparked a transformative change in his community. The small win of taking that first step led to a growing group of friends gathering each week to pray, support one another, and discuss their faith struggles.

Through this journey, Michael found that sharing his faith with others not only strengthened his own belief but also created a ripple effect of encouragement within his circle. The act of initiating that prayer group, which may have seemed trivial at first, became a cornerstone of his faith, offering a sense of belonging and purpose. This small victory, like a pebble dropped into a pond, sent out waves of positivity and connection that reverberated throughout his life.

As we reflect on the narratives of Sara and Michael, we begin to uncover the deeper significance of small victories. They are not merely checkpoints on a spiritual radar; they are moments of intentionality and faith that honor our journey, acknowledging our efforts as worthy of recognition. Each small win carries the potential to reinforce our trust in God, bolster our resilience, and remind us of the presence of grace in our lives.

In the face of life's demands, it is easy to overlook the subtle victories that contribute to our spiritual growth. The world often urges us to seek out grand achievements: a promotion at work, a public speaking engagement, or a significant milestone in our ministries. While these moments certainly deserve celebration, they can overshadow the quiet, daily victories that contribute to our overall journey of faith.

Think of the countless times we choose to respond with

patience rather than anger, to extend grace to those who may not deserve it, or to practice kindness even when it seems challenging. Each of these moments represents a small victory—a deliberate choice to embody faith in our actions. Celebrating these instances empowers us to acknowledge our progress and encourages us to continue making similar choices in the future.

To illuminate the importance of these small wins, let us revisit some powerful truths from Scripture. The Bible is brimming with narratives that emphasize the value of seemingly insignificant achievements. In Zechariah 4:10, we read, "Do not despise these small beginnings, for the Lord rejoices to see the work begin." This verse reminds us that, in the eyes of God, every step forward is valuable. The act of beginning, whether it is taking time for prayer or reaching out to a friend, is celebrated in the divine economy.

Moreover, in Luke 16:10, we find Jesus teaching the principle of faithfulness in small things: "Whoever can be trusted with very little can also be trusted with much." This verse speaks to the interconnectedness of small victories and greater achievements. Each small act of faithfulness lays the groundwork for larger opportunities. When we are faithful in minor matters, we prepare ourselves for more significant responsibilities in God's kingdom.

Recognizing the power of small victories also requires an intentional mindset shift. Often, we become preoccupied with future ambitions and significant goals, neglecting the present moment and the milestones already achieved. To break this cycle, we can adopt practical strategies to celebrate small victories in our daily lives.

First, consider keeping a "victory journal." At the end of each day, take a few moments to reflect on your day and jot down small wins that occurred. This practice can be as simple as recognizing a moment of patience you displayed or noting a prayer that was answered, however subtly. By documenting these moments, you create a tangible record of progress, reinforcing the value of small victories over time.

Secondly, make it a habit to share your small wins with others. Whether through a group chat with friends or during family dinner conversations, the act of verbalizing these moments serves to celebrate and amplify their significance. Sharing victories not only encourages personal reflection but also strengthens community bonds as others are inspired by your journey. As a community, when we celebrate each other's small wins, we foster an environment of support and accountability that nurtures growth.

Additionally, consider creating rituals to honor small victories. This could involve setting aside time for gratitude prayer, lighting a candle to mark a moment of reflection, or enjoying a small treat after accomplishing a task. By creating rituals, you transform ordinary moments into opportunities for celebration and acknowledgment, deepening the appreciation for your journey of faith.

Another practical tip for honoring small victories is to challenge yourself with positive affirmations. As you recognize your achievements, take a moment to affirm your journey, perhaps by declaring, "I am moving forward in faith," or "Every step counts in my walk with Christ." This practice encourages internal validation, reinforcing the belief that your efforts are seen and valuable, regardless of their perceived magnitude.

In our faith journeys, it's essential to understand that every step we take is part of a greater narrative being woven by God. This perspective allows us to recognize that each small victory contributes to the unfolding of His purpose in our lives. Let us not forget the unique stories of triumph that shape our journeys.

Consider the wisdom of a mentor named Julia, who spent decades in ministry. Reflecting on her journey, she often shared how small victories in her ministry came from the most unexpected places—from a child remembering to pray, to a family finding hope after significant loss through a simple act of kindness. Each moment became a testament to perseverance and trust in God. Julia would say, "When we honor the small victories, we cultivate an environment where the miraculous can thrive."

As we move forward, let us carry this ethos into our daily lives. Embrace the understanding that your small victories matter—they mark your growth, strengthen your faith, and serve as reminders of God's faithfulness. Remember that the path to spiritual maturity is not always about monumental events; often, it is about the cumulative effect of small choices and consistent actions.

In closing, we are called to be mindful of our journeys and to celebrate the small victories along the way. As each character in our stories illustrates, the power of these moments is profound and life-changing. By recognizing and honoring our daily achievements, we invite greater awareness of God's movement in our lives.

This subchapter is a clarion call to rejoice in the small wins—the victories that form the foundation of our spiritual journey—and to acknowledge that every step forward, no matter how small, is worthy of celebration. Embrace the power of these moments, and allow them to propel you forward into deeper faith, resilience, and connection with God and your community. By celebrating the small victories, we cultivate grateful hearts, honor our journeys, and create a legacy of faith for those who follow.

Sharing Victories with Others

In our fast-paced lives, victories often come and go like fleeting moments, overshadowed by the demands of daily routines. Yet, within the tapestry of our faith journeys, every small win holds immense value, serving as stepping stones that guide us toward deeper connections with God and with each other. In this subchapter, we will explore the rich fabric of sharing victories within our faith communities, understanding how these communal celebrations not only strengthen our spiritual bonds but also uplift those around us.

At the heart of our faith lies an understanding that we are not meant to journey alone. The beauty of the Christian walk is interwoven with community, with shared joys and burdens connecting us to one another in profound ways. When we celebrate victories together, we step into an empowering rhythm of encouragement that reverberates through the hearts of all involved.

The Encourager, a character who has become emblematic of our exploration, stands as a beacon of light in this narrative. Throughout their journey, they've recognized that small victories—be it overcoming personal doubts, completing a difficult task, or achieving a goal—are worthy of celebration. One particularly poignant memory echoes in their mind; it was during a small family gathering where they decided to put this principle into action.

As friends and family circled around the table, enjoying a meal together, The Encourager raised a glass of sparkling juice to share a recent victory. "I've been struggling with my prayer life for some time," they began, their voice steady but filled with emotion. "But lately, I've been more consistent in setting aside time each morning to connect with God. It hasn't been easy, but I've felt a shift in my spirit."

The room filled with applause, not just for The Encourager's commitment, but also for the vulnerability shown in sharing this win. The smiles and nods that followed became a chorus of shared understanding, igniting a spark of joy. As various family members chimed in with their small victories—from mastering a new recipe to feeling more confident in their personal pursuits—the atmosphere shifted. What began as a simple meal transformed into a sacred celebration of life's achievements.

This moment exemplifies the heart of why we should share victories with others. Celebrating victories, no matter how small, fosters a sense of belonging within the community. It reinforces the idea that each person's journey is worthy of recognition and that the struggles we face are common. When we share our wins, we offer not just our stories but a mirror for others, inspiring them to recognize and celebrate their own small victories.

Communal celebrations of victory do more than uplift the moment. They create an environment where vulnerability and authenticity can thrive. In sharing our wins, we open the door for others to express their struggles and triumphs, cultivating a safe space for growth and encouragement. The Encourager recalls another occasion, this time at church. After a service, the pastor invited everyone to share one victory from the past week.

Nervousness initially filled the air, but as one voice stepped forward to recount a victory—going a week without giving in to a long-standing temptation—others began to follow suit.

Each sharing was met with enthusiastic applause, and laughter filled the sanctuary as stories unfolded. A woman spoke of her renewed commitment to daily devotionals, a teenager shared about making new friends at school, and a father beamed as he talked about rekindling his relationship with his teenage son. As these narratives rippled through the community, the sheer power of shared experiences was palpable. Each victory celebrated built a bridge, drawing the members closer together.

In another instance, The Encourager facilitated a small group gathering centered around sharing victories. They believed that holding space for gratitude could be transformative. Inviting friends, they encouraged each person to come prepared with a win to share. The result was a heartwarming evening filled with laughter, fellowship, and mutual encouragement. Each person took turns lighting up the room with their stories, creating an uplifting atmosphere where others felt inspired to reflect on their own journeys.

As we cultivate spaces for sharing victories, we invite opportunities for active participation in each other's growth. Establishing contexts where victories can be celebrated builds a shared sense of accountability. We eagerly engage in one another's lives, offering support in both triumphs and trials. The Encourager notes that just as victories are shared, so too are the stories of perseverance that led to those victories.

To create an environment that fosters celebrating victories, consider implementing these practical suggestions in your own faith community:

1. **Create Regular Sharing Sessions**: Designate times during gatherings, whether they are church services, small groups, or family meals, for sharing victories. This could be as simple as starting each meeting with a round of "victory moments," where everyone has the opportunity to reflect on their week.

2. **Develop a "Victory Wall"**: In physical spaces like churches or community centers, consider establishing a "Victory Wall" where members can post their wins on colorful papers. Visually celebrating achievements allows for a continuous reminder of God's work in the lives of individuals.

3. **Utilize Social Media**: Many communities engage online, so why not create a dedicated social media group where members feel free to share their victories? This creates a virtual space for encouragement throughout the

week, fostering connection beyond physical gatherings.

4. **Host Celebratory Gatherings**: Organize regular events focused on celebrating milestones within the community. This could be an evening of sharing testimonies, a picnic to recognize accomplishments, or themed gatherings where members can share their stories through art, music, or spoken word.

5. **Encourage One-on-One Sharing**: Equip members to celebrate victories on a more intimate level by encouraging one-on-one conversations. The Encourager often practices this with several close friends and has found that heart-to-heart celebrations can lead to deeper connections.

Through these methods, the act of sharing victories becomes a rhythmic practice within the community, encouraging an atmosphere that highlights growth, resilience, and hope.

As members impact one another with these celebrations, the ripple effects are profound. The Encourager witnessed an inspiring transformation within their group after consistent focus on celebrating small wins. One young woman who had initially struggled with feeling isolated and unnoticed began to shine. As she shared her recent achievements—such as taking a step to volunteer for a ministries project or even reaching out to classmates—others followed suit. The communal energy shifted as she felt the encouragement of her friends, and soon, she was beaming with confidence that influenced not only her personal life but also her faith journey.

This interplay of sharing victories in a supportive community creates an uplifting dynamism that fortifies faith. Rather than standing as lone islands, individuals become interwoven threads of an elaborate tapestry—each victory stitched together with love and encouragement.

The Encourager reflects on one particularly poignant moment when community bonds were further fortified through shared victories. A neighbor, who had faced tremendous adversity, found a new job after months of searching. In a heartfelt neighborhood gathering, the community came together to celebrate this achievement by organizing a small surprise party. They decorated their home, cooked their favorite dishes, and each person provided words of encouragement and testimony about the neighbor's journey. The joy radiating from that event became a defining moment, showing how shared victories weave our lives together.

When one part of the community succeeds, all are enriched by that triumph.

In moments of celebration, we create powerful testimonies about God's grace in our lives. Sharing our victories reflects a illuminating truth: that God is actively working in and through us. Together, these stories feed our collective faith, fostering resilience and deepening our trust in Him.

Ultimately, sharing victories invites us to break free from a culture that often emphasizes individual achievement over collective joy. In a world that promotes comparison and isolation, the practice of communal celebration serves as a counterbalance. By highlighting the importance of shared victories, we embody the love of Christ and express gratitude for His blessings.

So let us be a people who intentionally celebrate each small win, lifting one another up, and recognizing that in these moments, we are not just individuals navigating our journeys—we are a community, a family, bound together by faith and love, thriving on the victories that God pours into our lives.

As we continue to reflect on this theme, consider how you can infuse your own journey and community with the spirit of sharing victories. What victories are you grateful for, and how can you celebrate them with others? In taking the time to ponder these questions, you set the stage for profound growth, both personally and communally.

The road ahead is not always easy, but when we journey together, celebrating each stride, every small victory holds the power to transform lives, building faith and community as we walk hand in hand toward God's glorious future.

The Ripple Effect of Gratitude and Victory

In the vast tapestry of our lives, small victories often go unnoticed amidst the grandeur of our big dreams and aspirations. Yet, it is precisely these seemingly insignificant triumphs that, when cherished and celebrated, can reverberate through our communities and beyond, creating a ripple effect of gratitude and inspiration. Appreciating these moments is akin to throwing a small stone into a pond; the ripples expand, creating waves that touch and influence the heart of those around us.

As we pause to reflect on the small victories in our lives, we unveil the power they hold not just for ourselves, but also for our families, friends, and faith communities. Each triumph—no matter how minuscule—serves as a beacon of hope, illuminating the path for others on their faith journeys. The act of recognizing and celebrating these victories invites a tangible sense of gratitude that can inspire both the celebrant and the beholder.

Consider the story of a young woman named Grace, who, after years of feeling trapped in self-doubt, finally gathered the courage to join a local church group. A seemingly simple act, yet for Grace, it was monumental. She walked into that room, heart pounding, and for the first time, felt a sense of belonging. The warmth and acceptance she received from the group was not just a victory for her alone; it became a catalyzing moment for others there. As they saw Grace embrace her journey, even in her vulnerability, it inspired them to be transparent about their struggles too.

The ripple effect of Grace's victory extended far beyond her individual experience. It sparked conversations about self-acceptance and trust within the community, influencing others to acknowledge their own hesitant steps towards faith. Members who previously shied away from group discussions found the courage to share their faith stories, creating a nurturing environment where vulnerability was celebrated rather than judged.

When we reflect on our small victories, we begin to see a mosaic of experiences that connect us all. The stories we carry are not merely personal; they intertwine with the narratives of those around us. In sharing our moments of triumph, we invite others to see the divine in their struggles and victories, taking on a role that resembles the Encourager in our stories. Every small victory recognized and celebrated may very well become the stepping stone for someone else's breakthrough, fostering a cycle of support and inspiration.

Imagine the second ripple initiated by an intentional act of gratitude. When we express appreciation for our successes—be they big or small—we set a tone that encourages others to do the same. A simple "thank you" can transform a mundane interaction into a meaningful exchange. In our relationships, an acknowledgment of a partner's effort, a friend's support, or a colleague's triumph can weave a fabric of gratitude that envelops our surroundings.

Let us take a moment to visualize a community gathering in celebration of achievements. Each participant is invited to share a personal victory. As they share, laughter and tears intermingle, stories resonate, and hope is rekindled. This act of storytelling not only honors individual victories but also reinforces communal bonds. One by one, members share their stories, sparking affirmations and applause, and the room buzzes with energy. Each participant leaves feeling uplifted, cherished, and inspired to continue their faith journey with renewed vigor.

Furthermore, consider the potential for impact beyond our immediate circles. When we share our victories on larger platforms, whether through social media, blogs, or community newsletters, we have the opportunity to reach individuals we may never meet in person. The vulnerability and triumph in our stories can touch hearts that are miles away, offering inspiration to those feeling isolated or defeated in their own journeys.

Take, for instance, the impact of social media in today's world. An individuals who posts a personal victory—a successful completion of a project, a heartfelt recovery, or an answered prayer—can resonate with followers who may be experiencing similar struggles. A comment of encouragement on such a post can create a dialogue, nurturing connections between people of diverse backgrounds who find solace in shared experiences. One small victory celebrated online can lead to hopeful threads of conversation, forming a network of support that extends far beyond geographical boundaries.

In these digital spaces, we can foster environments of gratitude and inspiration through curated content that speaks to our communities. As we express thankfulness for the victories in our lives, we can challenge ourselves to highlight the victories of others—creating a sense of collective triumph. For instance, highlighting someone's progress in their faith journey, or acknowledging a friend who took the leap to pursue their calling, empowers them and reiterates the importance of recognizing one another's small victories. Such acts serve as reminders that we are all on unique paths, and in every journey, there is something to celebrate.

Reflecting on how we can uplift our communities through these victories requires intentionality. As part of our faith journey, we can integrate gratitude into our daily lives, subtly reminding ourselves to notice and appreciate the small wins that manifest each day. Journaling becomes a powerful tool in this practice. By taking time to jot down moments of gratitude or small triumphs, we cultivate a spirit of thankfulness that spills over into other areas of our lives.

Waking up and consciously recalling three victories from the previous day—be it successfully completing a workout, connecting meaningfully with a friend, or having a moment of peace—can set a positive tone for the day ahead. It shifts our focus from what is lacking to what is abundant, nurturing a heart full of gratitude. This simple act can be transformative, as the recognition of small wins reinforces our connection to God, grounding our faith in appreciation.

To inspire this practice further, let us explore reflective prompts that invite deeper introspection regarding our own small victories. These prompts can guide journaling sessions or group discussions, creating safe spaces for sharing and connection.

1. **What small victory have I experienced recently that I have overlooked?** Consider the little moments that may not appear significant at first glance but are, in reality, milestones in your faith journey.

2. **Who can I share my latest victory with, and how might doing so encourage them?** Reflect on how your story might serve as inspiration or encouragement for someone else.

3. **What practice of gratitude can I consciously implement in my daily life?** Identify a method to regularly acknowledge your own and others' small victories—be it

through journaling, verbal affirmations, or digital sharing.

4. **What roles have the small victories of others played in my own faith journey?** Think about how the victories of fellow believers have impacted your own path, reinforcing a sense of community and shared growth.

5. **What specific ways can I support and uplift those around me in celebrating their victories?** As you recognize the interconnectedness of your journey with others, consider practical steps to encourage communal celebrations of faith.

Through journaling and reflection, we become more attuned to the victories in our lives and the lives of those we encounter. This intentionality enables us to create a vibrant atmosphere of gratitude that extends outward, inviting more individuals to share in the joy of small successes.

In closing this subchapter, we remember that the power of recognizing small victories lies not only in their celebration for our own spiritual growth but also in their potential to inspire and uplift communities. The ripples we create can foster connection, hope, and encouragement in the hearts of those around us. We must commit to sharing these victories—both big and small—so that together, we can navigate our faith journeys hand in hand, continually supporting one another in our efforts to grow, inspire, and celebrate one another.

As we embrace the ripple effect of gratitude and victory, let us proceed with intention, creating echoes of hope and light that resonate through our lives and the lives of others. Each small step forward, every heartfelt celebration, reinforces the interconnectedness of our journeys and affirms the beauty of faith shared. Together, as we honor our small victories, we can pave the way for others to do the same, fostering a vibrant community characterized by gratitude, connection, and inspiration.

Trusting Beyond Understanding

Faith in Trials

The air was heavy with uncertainty, as if the very atmosphere was laden with doubt and fear. For both the Skeptic and the Woman at the Well, trials had been their unwelcome companions. Yet, it was in those moments of darkness, in the swirling storms of their lives, that they began to discover a faith that transcended their understanding.

For the Skeptic, life had always been about questions—for every answer he found, doubt lurked like a shadow, eager to drag him back into a sea of uncertainty. This constant battle waged inside him created a relentless tension, one that was only magnified during the hardest times of his life. When his career crumbled, leaving him feeling isolated and lost, the world he had built, predicated on logic and reason, suddenly felt unstable. Everything he thought he knew was challenged, and he found himself grappling with despair. Friends who had once rallied around him started to drift away, unseen currents of worry and judgment pulling them from his sphere. In these moments of uncertainty, the Skeptic often found himself staring into the abyss, wrestling with the weight of his unanswered questions.

But there was a pivotal moment that changed everything for him. Reflecting on a solitary night where he felt utterly abandoned, he stumbled across a passage in the book of Proverbs: "Trust in the Lord with all your heart, and lean not on your own understanding." As he contemplated these words, an unexpected sense of clarity washed over him. Aimlessly trusting God, when all he had known was self-reliance, felt foreign. Yet, in that moment, the fog of doubt began to lift, revealing the first glimmers of hope beneath.

Meanwhile, the Woman at the Well had her own trials, so

profound that they ran deep like a jagged wound. Her past was riddled with mistakes and moments of shame, leading her to find solace in the isolation of midday water collection. Each trip to the well brought with it the burden of societal judgment, whispering past mistakes into her ears like a cruel symphony. Yet, it was also at this well where she encountered Jesus—a moment that would alter the fabric of her existence. The truth she had evaded crashed into her heart as she listened to Him speak, illuminating her life like the dawn after a long night.

In her trials, she, too, had grappled with her understanding of faith. It was through her encounter with Jesus that she learned to trust in someone greater than the sum of her experiences. Here was a man who knew her story, her hurts, and yet offered her grace. The very act of trusting beyond her brokenness became the foundation for her spiritual rebirth.

As she recalled the urgency in His voice, "If you knew the gift of God and who it is that asks you for a drink," she felt as though the burdens of her past began to lift. Trusting Jesus amidst her societal rejection transformed her shame into testimony, offering hope to the very people who had shunned her. She recognized that her trials were not merely chains binding her, but stepping stones leading her towards a profound understanding of God's grace.

The Skeptic watched this transformative journey with renewed interest. He could see the Woman at the Well as she interacted with others after her encounter with Christ. She moved with an aura of confidence, radiating love and compassion. Someone who had once felt the sting of public scrutiny was now a beacon of hope, sharing her story and, in turn, igniting faith in others. This was not just belief; rather, it was a testament to the power of trusting God through trials.

Their intertwining stories reveal that faith is not just about a singular moment of clarity; it is also about embracing the journey—a path often clouded by doubt, questions, and unforeseen challenges. It is in these seemingly insurmountable trials that faith is forged. Scripture reminds us, "Consider it pure joy, my brothers and sisters, whenever you face trials of many kinds, because you know that the testing of your faith produces perseverance" (James 1:2-3).

What trials has the reader faced? Perhaps it was a sudden job loss, a health scare, or a familial breakdown, each trial resonating differently for everyone. The weight of those challenges can seem unbearable, leaving individuals feeling stranded amidst the tempestuous waves of life. Yet, just as the Skeptic and the Woman at the Well discovered, it is in those moments of uncertainty that trust in God is paramount.

Trust does not mean the absence of questions or doubt; rather, it is the resolve to continue moving forward in faith despite them. When faced with difficulty, the Skeptic learned to harness the courage found in vulnerability. He began to open his heart in prayer, seeking a connection with God that surpassed his need for answers. That transformative act of reaching out changed the nature of their relationship. He felt God's presence, and in doing so, begun to unravel the intricacies of his faith.

The Woman at the Well similarly faced her doubts head-on. After meeting Jesus, she was propelled back to her community, her heart aflame with a newfound purpose. Yet, she wrestled with the fear of rejection once more. Would they accept this changed woman? Would they listen to her? Her decision to confront these lingering doubts was rooted in a deep recognition of the miracle she had experienced. In every step towards her past, she found strength in the truth she had uncovered through Christ.

Trials serve as profound teachers in the faith journey, but they can feel debilitating when faced alone. "And let us consider how we may spur one another on toward love and good deeds, not giving up meeting together, as some are in the habit of doing, but encouraging one another" (Hebrews 10:24-25). The Skeptic turned to the Woman at the Well, and together they found strength in communal support, particularly during moments filled with uncertainty. The shared testimonies of overcoming trials bonded them, inspiring courage as they navigated their respective journeys.

As the Skeptic reflected on his situation, he recalled the words inscribed in the Bible: "For I know the plans I have for you, declares the Lord, plans to prosper you and not to harm you, plans to give you hope and a future" (Jeremiah 29:11). These verses bolstered his resolve; trusting God meant allowing room for His plans, however different from what he had once envisioned for himself. Slowly, he learned that understanding is not always a prerequisite for faith— rather, faith can often lead to a deeper understanding and fulfillment of life.

When he started to be open about his struggles, he found others were encouraged to share their experiences as well. Names and faces of support began to emerge—a mentor from the church, friends who had also faced challenges, and even a stranger whose journey mirrored his own. This network of believers became a lifeline during the storms he faced, reminding him that he was not alone in his journey.

For the Woman at the Well, community was a part of her healing process. The reception of her story created ripples in the lives of others. She became an advocate for the very faith she had once shunned, eager to invite others to experience the same transformative love that had shifted her world. It became evident to her that each trial she faced was not just her own; they were collective experiences that bound the community together in their faith.

Scripture continuously invites us to seek help from one another in our trials. Galatians 6:2 encourages believers to "Carry each other's burdens, and in this way you will fulfill the law of Christ." The Skeptic and the Woman at the Well sought strength and companionship from those who walked alongside them in faith. Encouragement emerged as a powerful force, reminding each of them that they were part of a larger story, one intertwined with God's overarching narrative of grace, redemption, and love.

Even amidst these encouraging stories, doubt still lingered. The Skeptic grappled with setbacks, moments where the questions seemed insurmountable once again. Yet in these moments, he learned to cling to scripture dearly. Romans 8:28 resonated in his heart, reminding him that "And we know that in all things God works for the good of those who love him, who have been called according to his purpose." The reassurance that God could take even the messiest situations and weave them into something beautiful became a lifeline amidst turbulent waters.

The Woman at the Well, too, faced moments of doubt. In her new role as an evangelist, she dealt with naysayers, skeptics who refused to see her as anything other than her past mistakes. Yet, as she recounted her story, she found strength in revealing her vulnerability before God. In prayer, she laid her fears bare before Him, finding solace in the truth that God saw her as worthy of love and redemption.

In learning to confront their trials and trusting beyond their understanding, both characters discovered a sense of resilience. They learned that trials were not barriers but bridges to deeper faith. Psalm 34:17-18 illuminated their path: "The righteous cry out, and the Lord hears them; he delivers them from all their troubles. The Lord is close to the brokenhearted and saves those who are crushed in spirit."

For readers grappling with their own trials, it is crucial to recognize that God is present amidst them, often unveiling His plans when they least expect it. This journey is not merely about seeking answers but about cultivating a heart willing to trust, to step into the unknown while believing that God is at work.

As the trials of life come—whether they manifest as unexpected job losses, family issues, health crises, or personal battles—remember the stories of the Skeptic and the Woman at the Well. Both faced challenges that tested their faith, urging them to lean into God's promises. Their journeys remind us that in the midst of uncertainty, we can choose to trust, even beyond our understanding.

Incorporating their stories into our own narratives provides strength and hope as we navigate life's unpredictable waters. As we grapple with our trials, let us join together in community, sharing burdens and celebrating victories. Trusting God amidst life's struggles cultivates a profound sense of purpose, filling the void left by doubt and fear.

As we wrap up this exploration of faith amidst trials, let us remember the truth that in trusting God beyond understanding, we find hope, resilience, and ultimately, a deeper relationship with Him. Embrace your trials; allow them to lead you to greater faith. David reassures us in Psalm 30:5, "Weeping may stay for the night, but rejoicing comes in the morning." The shadows will not last forever; the dawn of renewed faith is on the horizon. Seek Him in your trials, trust Him through each storm, and witness the miraculous transformation that can occur when we let go of understanding, clinging instead to the One who knows our hearts completely.

Finding Strength in Vulnerability

In the quiet moments of life, when chaos surrounds us and uncertainty looms, we often find ourselves at a crossroads—one that leads to either withdrawal into our shells or the courageous act of opening our hearts. As I reflect on my own journey, I am struck by the profound strength that comes from vulnerability. It is in these raw, unfiltered moments where we allow ourselves to be seen, to be known by God, that we experience a deepening connection that transcends our understanding.

I recall a particularly challenging season in my life when the weight of despair felt insurmountable. It was a time when I found myself grappling with doubt, fear, and a sense of isolation. The burdens I carried were heavy, and I often retreated inward, thinking I had to navigate these storms alone. Yet, every attempt to conceal my struggles only deepened my sense of hopelessness. It was in a moment of desperation, lying on my bed, tears cascading down my cheeks, that I realized I could no longer bear the weight of it all.

In that vulnerable moment, I fell to my knees and cried out to God. I let go of the pretense of having it all together and instead embraced my reality—my fears, my frustrations, and my failures. I poured out my heart, laying bare the conflict within me. And as I did, I felt the heaviness begin to lift. It was as if a light had pierced through the darkness, illuminating my path and reminding me that I was not alone—the Creator of the universe was right there with me, inviting me to share my innermost thoughts.

Being vulnerable before God allowed me to confront the very things that had been holding me captive. It led to a deeper understanding of who I am and whose I am. God did not reject me for my doubts or my fears. Instead, I felt accepted, loved, and embraced. The weight of shame that often accompanies our struggles began to dissolve, and I realized that my imperfections were not barriers to God's love but rather openings to experience His grace more profoundly.

What I discovered in this process was that vulnerability is not a sign of weakness; rather, it is a testament to our humanity. It is an invitation to engage authentically with God and others. When we expose our weaknesses and ask for help, we dismantle the illusion of control and perfection that often isolates us. In our humanness, we find connection—not just with God, but with one another.

As I delved deeper into this understanding, I began to reflect on the stories within the Scriptures. One that stands out vividly is the story of David. Despite his flaws and failures—adultery, murder, and in many ways, a typical human being—David's vulnerability before God is striking. He was unafraid to pour out his heart in the Psalms, expressing his fears, joys, regrets, and hopes. Psalms like 34:18 echo the sentiment that God is close to the brokenhearted and saves those who are crushed in spirit. David's openness led not only to an intimate relationship with God but also to a legacy of faith that continues to resonate centuries later.

The beauty of being vulnerable is that it fosters an environment where healing can flourish. As we familiarize ourselves with the concept of vulnerability, it's essential to recognize the power of sharing our experiences within our faith communities. I have witnessed incredible transformations in individuals and groups when they collectively embrace their vulnerabilities. Testimonies of struggle and pain can pave the way for communal healing and restoration. In those circles of shared experiences, the body of Christ can operate like a wellspring of trust and support.

I remember a small group I was part of during a particularly trying time. Each week, as we gathered in someone's living room, we shared our burdens and prayed for one another. Those evenings became sacred spaces—not just for sharing successes but for revealing our trials. We learned that it was okay to not be okay. There was freedom in confessing our fears and uncertainties. As we supported one another, I felt the bonds of our community deepen. Our shared vulnerabilities created a tapestry of strength that encouraged us all.

Reflection is a powerful tool for cultivating vulnerability in our lives. As we take the time to examine our own hearts and experiences, we illuminate the pathways that lead us to deeper trust with God. Here are some practical exercises to help you engage with this transformative practice:

1. **Journaling Vulnerably**: Set aside time each week to write honestly in a journal. Allow yourself to explore your emotions—what you're feeling, what fears you might be wrestling with, and where you see God's hand at work in your struggles. Don't shy away from details; instead, write as if you're expressing your thoughts to a trusted friend. This openness can lead to profound insights and healing.

2. **Prayer of Honesty**: Craft a prayer that reflects your current emotional state, regardless of how fragmented or uncertain it may seem. You might begin by acknowledging your struggles and then invite God into those spaces, asking for clarity, strength, and understanding. This act of honesty can bridge the gap between your heart and the heart of God.

3. **Accountability Partner**: Find a friend or mentor within your faith community who you trust. Share your vulnerabilities and struggles with them, and invite them to do the same. In this reciprocal relationship, you can hold space for each other's journeys, offering encouragement and support as needed.

4. **Meditation on Scripture**: Choose a passage of Scripture that speaks to vulnerability, such as 2 Corinthians 12:9,

which reads, "But he said to me, 'My grace is sufficient for you, for my power is made perfect in weakness.'" Reflect on this passage. Consider how God's strength is made manifest in your weaknesses, and pray for the grace to embrace that aspect of your faith journey.

5. **Engaging in Community**: Participate in your faith community's small groups or outreach programs. Create space for vulnerability by sharing your experiences with others, inviting them to open up in turn. You might be surprised by the connections that develop when you allow yourself to be seen.

Embracing vulnerability before God is an act that transcends the confines of our struggles. It opens avenues of connection and trust that have the potential not only to strengthen our faith but also to transform our relationships with others. Through vulnerability, we invite God into our weaknesses and step into a reality filled with hope and renewal.

As we navigate the complexities of life and faith, we must remind ourselves that vulnerability is a beautiful bridge that connects us to God and the community. It invites us to relinquish the burdens we were never meant to carry alone and to discover the richness of God's grace.

In the moments when life feels overwhelming and the temptation to retreat into silence stirs within us, let us choose vulnerability instead. Let us lean into our imperfections and reach out to God, trusting that it is through these openings that His love and strength flow abundantly.

In the tapestry of our faith journeys, vulnerability is a thread that weaves connections deeply anchored in trust. And as we continue to explore the depths of our struggles and embrace the vulnerability that comes with being human, we will discover a faith that can withstand any storm—one that boldly declares that we are not alone, for God is with us every step of the way.

Through the lens of vulnerability, we find not just strength in our weaknesses but a thriving hope that propels us forward in faith. The flickering flame of trust, ignited in those intimate moments before God, shines brightly, guiding us through every uncertainty with reassurance and love. Let us fully embrace this divine invitation to be vulnerable, trusting that it will lead us not only to greater intimacy with God but also to a faith that goes beyond understanding—a faith that radiates strength in the face of life's challenges.

The Hope Beyond Understanding

As the sun began to set, casting a golden hue across the landscape, Maria found herself standing at the threshold of what once felt like an insurmountable wall. It was the wall of grief, a towering barrier that had risen abruptly when she lost her husband to a sudden illness. Just weeks prior, they had been planning for their future, making dreams that now felt shattered and distant. The ache in her heart was profound, a mixture of disbelief and despair that seemed to envelop her completely.

In the days following his passing, darkness threatened to consume her. Friends and family offered their sympathy, and yet, Maria felt isolated in a world that moved on without her. She questioned everything—her faith, the love she believed was eternal, and the promise of hope that had been a part of her life for so long. Late at night, when silence settled like a heavy blanket, doubt crept in, whispering devastating questions: "Why did this happen? Where is God in my suffering?"

It was in this profound place of sorrow that Maria encountered a community that would impact her life deeply—a small group at her church that gathered weekly to explore faith, scripture, and real-life struggles. Despite her reluctance, one rainy evening she made her way to their meeting, the drive filled with trepidation. What could they possibly say that would ease the emptiness she felt?

As the evening unfolded, the group shared their experiences, struggles, and moments where they felt God's presence amid their trials. One member, James, spoke of his battle with anxiety, detailing how he had come to find peace in prayer, even when the storms raged within. Another, Sarah, shared her journey through infertility, expressing her painful longing for a child and the hopelessness that hovered over her for years. Yet, each testimony was marked by a common thread—their faith had not abandoned them in their darkest hours.

Maria found herself tearing up as she listened, the vulnerability they shared resonating deep within her. Each story illuminated a flicker of hope, a reminder that amidst the turmoil, God was present, offering light in the deepening shadows. It wasn't about circumstances miraculously changing; it was about the quiet assurance that God walks with His people through suffering. With each story, the darkness that had wrapped around her heart began to loosen its grip, making room for light and hope.

As weeks turned into months, Maria continued attending the group. She began journaling her thoughts and prayers, pouring out her frustrations to God, her heart slowly opening to the possibility that hope was not just a distant dream but something tangible to experience even in her pain. She recalled a particular night, felt the weight of loss heavily upon her; she prayed the simple words, "Lord, I trust you with this darkness."

In that moment, she experienced a shift—a flicker of hope ignited by something beyond understanding. Life was still difficult, the heartache remained, but she sensed a lift in her spirit, an assurance that she was held in God's palms, even amid despair. That evening, she discovered an inner strength to face another day, believing that perhaps there would be moments of joy again.

The Bible is filled with stories that display God's faithfulness even when circumstances seem dire. One such story was that of Paul and Silas, imprisoned for their faith. When unjustly thrown into the dark confines of a cell, their circumstances looked bleak. Yet, in the darkest hour, they chose to sing praises to God. Acts 16:25-26 recounts how they prayed and sang hymns at midnight, and as they did, the foundations of the prison were shaken, and the doors were opened. Paul and Silas' faith turned their prison of despair into a sanctuary of hope, demonstrating that even in difficult places, trust in God can lead to miraculous outcomes. Their story transcends time, reminding us that hope is never lost, even in the most confining circumstances.

In reflecting on her own life, Maria felt like Paul and Silas that night—imprisoned by pain but choosing to lift her eyes to the heavens. Trusting God in those dark nights, she began to realize, opened her heart to a new perspective on hope, one that did not rely solely on her understanding of her circumstances but one rooted deeply in faith.

As Maria's journey matured, she began to reach out to others who faced their own trials. One day, a friend from the group reached out, seeking comfort after losing her job. Maria, filled with compassion, shared her experience of grief and how she discovered hope through the embrace of faith and community. Together, they prayed, seeking solace and strength in God's promises. Maria found herself transformed in this interaction—her pain was becoming purpose. By sharing her story, she illuminated hope for another, just as she had received it.

It's a cycle of hope that defies human reasoning. In 2 Corinthians 1:3-4, Paul writes, "Blessed be the God and Father of our Lord Jesus Christ, the Father of mercies and God of all comfort, who comforts us in all our affliction, so that we may be able to comfort those who are in any affliction." This scripture reminded Maria that her journey through grief wasn't just for her enlightenment but a vehicle through which she could offer hope to others navigating their valleys.

Hope comes alive when we lean on one another, shared through stories, prayers, and acts of kindness. It solidifies our connections and inspires us to look beyond our circumstances. Community is a tapestry of intertwining stories, each thread representing a struggle embraced with faith. Every person holds a piece of hope, waiting to be shared to light the path for another.

In the months that followed, Maria and her church community organized a support group for others dealing with grief and loss. Each week, they gathered to share stories, support one another, and seek God's guidance. Maria served not merely as a participant but also as a beacon of hope, illustrating how faith had served her as a lifeline. Through tears and laughter, they discovered the beauty found in vulnerability, the safety in sharing burdens, and the powerful impact of bearing one another's weights.

The transformative nature of hope became evident in those sacred meetings. Sarah found peace in her faith and continued to seek joy, understanding that her worth wasn't tied to motherhood alone. James slowly worked through his anxiety, learning to relinquish control, embracing the moments when trust felt heavy. The community bloomed, united by their struggles and the belief that even in their pain, God provided a profound support system often seen in each other.

Such transformations are echoed in our own lives, waiting to be uncovered amidst times of turmoil. Reflecting on moments of despair can illuminate paths towards growth, shining a light on how clinging to hope can lead to profound change. We aren't promised an easy journey. However, when faced with trials, holding on to God's promises offers us the hope we need to endure.

Perhaps today, you find yourself in a season of struggle and uncertainty, wondering if there truly is a light at the end of the tunnel. Know this: Our circumstances may seem overpowering, but God invites us to trust Him beyond our understanding. Hope, although often cloaked in shadows, is reachable.

Let us take a moment to reflect and seek God. Perhaps you can close your eyes now, invite honesty into your heart, and surrender the burdens you carry. Imagine laying them at the feet of Jesus— each worry, every pain, and the uncertainties of life. Pray this with me:

"Dear Lord, I come before you today acknowledging the weight I carry. I find myself in times of darkness, struggling to hold on to hope. I trust You, even when my understanding falters. Teach me to see the light in my struggles, reminding me that you promise to walk alongside me, illuminating my path. Help me endure, strengthen my faith, and let hope blossom within my heart. Give me courage to reach out to others, to share this journey of faith, and to be a source of hope for those around me. Thank you, Lord, for your abiding love and faithfulness. In Jesus' name, Amen."

As you journey through life's challenges, remember that trusting God, especially when understanding fails, opens the door to hope. The light you carry can illuminate the lives of others. The struggles you face may transform into stories of triumph, showcasing how faith can rise from the ashes and build bridges to connect hearts.

In moments when despair fills the air, take a moment to pause, reflect, and reach out for help. Trust in God will provide a guiding light, even in the darkest of nights. Hold on to hope—

breathe it in, share it, and let it flourish in your life and the lives of others. Together, let us illuminate the world one life at a time, for in doing so, we reflect the beautiful promise of God's unwavering light, shining brightly amidst darkness.

Thank You, Faithful Readers

As we reach the final pages of this devotional, my heart fills with gratitude for each and every one of you who embarked on this journey with me. Thank you for allowing these reflections to enter your spirit and for immersing yourselves in the beauty of daily faith exploration. It's been an incredible ride, hasn't it? Together, we've traversed the highs and lows of trusting God, dug deep into scripture, and unearthed rich treasures of insight that can transform how we view our daily lives.

I hope you're leaving these pages not just with knowledge, but with a renewed passion for deepening your relationship with God. Remember, faith isn't about having all the answers; it's about the journey of trust, surrender, and community that we weave together. Celebrate every step you take from here on out—each small victory counts!

As you reflect on 'The Gift of Patience' or how to 'Overcome Doubt', keep those lessons close to your heart. Carry those moments of prayer with you, and let them guide you even in challenging times. Whenever uncertainty arises, remember the power of trusting beyond what you can see. And when in doubt, reach for the community of believers around you; together, we can soar higher than we could alone.

Let the joy of gratitude ignite your daily life. Cultivating a thankful heart isn't just a task; it's a way of seeing the world through the lens of faith. Formulate your own gratitude practices, and let the seemingly ordinary moments fill you with awe and reverence for God's presence. Don't let this journey end here! Make it a part of your lifestyle, and encourage others to join in as well!

Your faith journey is so incredibly valuable. Share your learnings, stories, and reflections with those in your circle. Inspire, uplift, and challenge each other to trust God more profoundly. Together, we can cultivate a vibrant community of faith that impacts not just ourselves, but the world around us, creating a ripple effect that could resonate far beyond our imaginations.

As I part with you, remember that this devotional was crafted with love, intention, and hope. I truly believe that every reader has the capacity to deepen their faith and transform their relationship with God, and I can't wait for you to experience the wondrous things He has in store for you. May your heart be filled with courage, trust, and hope as you step into each day ahead. Here's to the vibrant journey that awaits you!

With all my heart Christian Ceasar